D0477261

EMMA
RADUCANU
WHEN TENNIS CAME HOME

MIKE DICKSON

HODDER &
STOUGHTON

First published in Great Britain in 2022 by Hodder & Stoughton
An Hachette UK company

1

Copyright © Mike Dickson 2022

A CIP catalogue record for this title is available from the British Library

Hardback ISBN 978 1 399 70555 4
Trade Paperback ISBN 978 1 399 70875 3
eBook ISBN 978 1 399 70556 1

Typeset in Warnock Pro by Hewer Text UK Ltd, Edinburgh
Printed and bound in Great Britain by Clays Ltd, Elcograf S.p.A.

Hodder & Stoughton policy is to use papers that are natural, renewable
and recyclable products and made from wood grown in sustainable
forests. The logging and manufacturing processes are expected to
conform to the environmental regulations of the country of origin.

Hodder & Stoughton Ltd
Carmelite House
50 Victoria Embankment
London EC4Y 0DZ

www.hodder.co.uk

CONTENTS

PROLOGUE |

Back in the UK it was 11.09 p.m. on what is known as 9/11 in New York. In the city where those numbers have such resonance, it was past six o'clock in the early evening when Emma Raducanu walked up to the service line, having a third championship point to win the US Open. And then she served and the ball came off her racket like the crack of a rifle. 'I was like, "If I'm going to make it, this is going to be the time." I drove my legs up to that ball-toss like never before. I landed it,' she said later, once the mayhem had subsided.

At eighteen years old she had won a Grand Slam, as a qualifier. There had been ten matches, no tiebreaks and no sets dropped. Over the course of the main draw she conceded thirty-four games, just two more than the great Serena Williams had lost seven years earlier when she cut through the US Open field like a threshing machine.

Inevitably we reached for sporting comparisons, and for explanations of this extraordinary turn of events in 2021, but none were entirely satisfactory. Leicester City winning the Premier League was thrown in, as was the parallel of a non-league team winning the FA Cup. This was, though, a triumph all of its own. The stars had, most definitely, aligned for someone who was relatively fresh from sitting their A-levels, yet it was not a fluke, nor was it a fairy tale. Neither is possible at a Grand Slam in the highly professionalised world of tennis.

One intangible thing stood out in the wake of this episode: everyone, almost without exception, from within the parish of the pro game was delighted for Emma Raducanu. In a highly competitive world, where Schadenfreude is a readily available doubles partner, people were genuinely pleased for this teenager from Kent. That was the reaction from within the confines of the sport. On the outside, the public instantly took to this most relatable champion's wide-eyed wonderment, her willingness to engage with courtside fans immediately after matches, something that still had a novelty value to it.

Had she really come from nowhere prior to Wimbledon, as was the understandable public perception? She had not. Within the game an exceptionally bright future had been predicted for some time, although nobody could be sure when she would arrive. You might have described her, in the words of the late American politician Donald Rumsfeld, as a known unknown.

A confluence of circumstances had led to her emerging earlier in the summer seemingly from the blue, much of it related to the effects of the pandemic on the tennis circuit. One tour staffer later recalled that just eleven weekends before, on the eve of Wimbledon, she had been offered up for interview to the press and host broadcasters, and there had been only one taker. No disrespect intended, there were just many more targets around to speak to – and we were also in the throes of a major international football tournament at the time.

What I hope this book will do is join many of the dots in the story of how someone came to burst from obscurity to global fame. There were many people who helped and worked with her along the way – I am aware that this is not an exhaustive account of them all, but hopefully a fair cross-section. I am grateful to those who spoke about Emma, both attributably and unattributably.

Above all, it is a story of one remarkably resourceful and talented individual. In pure tennis terms, it also illustrates that the ever-present ingredient in making a champion is a support-ive and ambitious family. That will always be more important than elaborate or expensive national systems. As the player, borrowing from a song, put it herself on one heady night in New York: 'My dad said to me, "You're even better than your dad thought."'

With Wimbledon cancelled, the still little-known Emma Raducanu takes advantage of one of the few opportunities for competitive tennis in 2020 – at the National Tennis Centre in Roehampton.

1

SUNDERLAND

An indoor tennis complex on the outskirts of Sunderland in February – it is not to be confused with the manicured lawns of Wimbledon on a balmy summer's afternoon.

Yet the chances are that any young tennis player with the ambition to make it to SW19 will have to pass through this kind of place and the type of tournament it hosts. The welcome is warm at the Silksworth Tennis and Wellness Spa, but you would be left in no doubt that football is the main preoccupation in these parts, especially when the onset of spring is still a distant rumour.

It was here that I ventured in February 2020, to a remote outpost of the professional game that was hosting a 'Futures' event, what constitutes the lowest level of the international tour. So had nearly 100 tennis players in all, male and female, competing for £38,000 in prize money, and the equally precious currency of world ranking points. (For the uninitiated, there are basically four tiers to the official circuit in ascending order: Futures, Challenger, the main WTA and ATP Tours, and then the Grand Slams. Some players supplement their competitive earnings by turning out at events which do not carry ranking points. These would include the domestic British Tour and UK Pro League, or the highly competitive club leagues in countries like France and Germany.)

The lower rungs are not standard territory for those who write about the sport; they would not be considered fertile ground for the kind of stories that are going to knock football or rugby's Six Nations off the back page in winter.

There is usually a specific motive for attending somewhere like Sunderland. In my case, it was to speak with Marcus Willis, one of the more recognisable members of British tennis's rank and file. Marcus once enjoyed one of those brushes with overnight national fame that, every now and then, sees someone step forward from the chorus line into a starring role at Wimbledon. Having won three rounds of the pre-qualifying event of 2016 (open only to domestic players), he had won three more in the full qualifying competition to make the main draw proper. He progressed to the second round, where he played Roger Federer on the Centre Court. Marcus had quit the game two years later, but now, with his generous frame and fast hands, he had decided to make a comeback as a doubles specialist.

Word of this had reached me, and he was happy to do an interview at his first tournament back on home soil. Time spent with Marcus is rarely wasted, usually being a source of a few good quotes and lively anecdotes. Besides that there is, journalistically, an element of speculating to accumulate in travelling to somewhere like Sunderland. And far beneath the shimmering glamour of the Grand Slams, this is where you get to feel the essence of the professional game.

With its skeleton crew of umpires and line judges, and an audience consisting of a few diehard anoraks, coaches and family members, in its own way this kind of lower-level tournament is where victory and defeat really matters to players: the difference between constructing a career and not making it. You can hear the anguished cries echo around the hall as the dream dies with each setback, while it is also where hope springs eternal. The fist-pumps seem to mean more. This kind of week is not just another well-remunerated stop on a tour in which there is always next week – tomorrow never comes for many of the defeated at a venue like Sunderland.

The field for this event in early 2020 was a fairly typical mix. If anything, it was slightly stronger than you might usually find for a Futures, because Britain has the reputation for running well-organised tournaments. The Lawn Tennis Association stages them more smoothly than most nations and is prepared to take the inevitable financial hit, as they always run at a loss. Players from overseas know that a Futures in the UK will have a sound infrastructure and some half-decent accommodation at local hotels or bed and breakfasts.

So Sunderland had a smattering of older players trying to rebuild their careers, as well as younger ones trying to forge their path. Igor Sijsling, a thirty-two-year-old Dutchman once ranked 52, was in the former category, while on the women's side there was his compatriot Richel Hogenkamp, who had once seen the inside of the top 100, and Croatian Jana Fett, another who once achieved a double-digit ranking. Of the young British players on show, Surrey's Jack Draper was the most highly touted, already doing enough to suggest that he ought to be aiming very high.

And then there was the seventeen-year-old schoolgirl from the Kent/London borders, Emma Raducanu.

She had been on my radar for some time, particularly since she began winning such events at the age of fifteen. We had seen her perform in a few of the junior Grand Slams at home and overseas although, unlike some, she had never been a regular fixture in these draws. She had done enough in the mini-Majors to persuade me to the outside courts on a couple of occasions, but never sufficient to warrant coverage of any depth. If memory served correctly, she had come in after one match in New York, in 2018, to speak to a couple of us briefly after one of the early rounds.

Now she was in the canteen at Silksworth, having just finished practice. John Morris, the agent who was working with her for the multinational IMG management agency, was up there for a couple of days on scouting business and, amid the pleasant informality of these settings, he came over with Emma to join Marcus and me as we chatted over coffee. In truth, it is difficult to remember much about the content of our four-way conversation, and certainly no notes were taken.

What is easy to recall is the subject arising of a rather worrying virus that had emerged in Asia and was, somewhat alarmingly, starting to appear in European ski resorts. Even then, in February, it felt more like a distant roll of thunder. Knowing that Emma was combining tennis with continuing education, we talked about her A-levels, and there was no doubt she was taking them very seriously. My interest was already piqued, because when her name had arisen before with John he had confidently predicted that one day she would make the world's top ten. A coach of my acquaintance, David Felgate, had said something similar, but cautioned that patience would be required as she was giving equal priority to academic pursuits. Quite a prediction, but as neither was prone to go over the top about young players, their view had definitely been filed away in the memory cabinet.

Whatever her physical potential as a player, by the time she politely took her leave from the table you could not help being struck by how much more accomplished she was than most teenagers you might come across in those circumstances. How she had listened, engaged and, for example, not been distracted by her phone. Someone, you suspected, who would end up doing well in life whatever path she chose.

If there was any scepticism on my part about the lofty forecasts of her tennis potential, it was due to a familiarity with the numbers game in play when it comes to young tennis prospects, especially those from the UK. Anyone with a mathematical mind – someone like Emma Raducanu, in fact – would know that most of the players that week in Sunderland would never emerge from the quagmire of the tour's lowest levels and reach the world's top 100. In a global individual sport it is a very difficult mark to achieve.

Statistics bear this out. In 2019, the last undisrupted year before the pandemic, there were 557 tournaments staged globally for women alone as part of what is known as the ITF (International Tennis Federation) Tour. Offering computer points, these lead to around 1,600 players having an official world ranking on the female side of the game, and closer to 2,000 on the men's. According to the ITF, of the girls who make the hotly contested top 100 of the junior rankings, only 19 per cent will ever go on to see the senior top 100 at any stage of their adult careers. For the boys it is less than half that.

You will hear a lot about making the top 100 in tennis, a magical benchmark for reasons that go beyond its round-number significance. It also happens to be almost the exact cut-off that guarantees a player entry into all four of the Grand Slam singles events, and is therefore the level at which you can begin to make a decent income. It is more than just some mythical number. It is the point when you can start being more self-reliant, rather than going cap in hand to sponsors, governing bodies and parents. The Slams are the tournaments where winning a couple of rounds makes you not just a name but some serious money. Even losing in all four first rounds at the Majors in a calendar year guarantees someone around £150,000 in cash, a significant baseline from which to build.

The hard fact is, however, that the British game rarely produces individuals who achieve this status for any length of time. Tennis in the UK is a strange phenomenon, a cross between the Promised Land (Wimbledon) and the Bermuda Triangle of racket sports, a place where a lot of talent seems to get swallowed up and disappear.

An approximate rule of thumb would be that, over recent decades, the British system (excluding those who have been substantially developed elsewhere) has wholly produced a cast-iron top-100 woman once every five years, and a top-100 man every six. As for the general intake at Sunderland that week, wherever they were from, for the large majority the Silksworth Tennis and Wellness Spa would be about as good as it gets. There would be some great life experiences and lessons, a free US college education perhaps, but a lucrative long-term career in the big time would remain just a dream.

The consensus about Raducanu among the cognoscenti was that she would, assuredly, be an exception to the rule: most definitely a product of the British tennis system, rooted in the London commuter territory of Bromley, and destined for a career playing in the great cathedrals of the sport.

Sitting over our Americanos in this north-eastern tennis outpost, however, it could not have entered anyone's heads that, barely fifteen months later, in 2021, she would become an overnight star at Wimbledon – eclipsing, even, the brief fairy tale lived out by one of the four at our table. And as for winning the US Open eighteen months on . . .

That view appeared to be shared by Emma herself. As we shall see, she did actually play a limited number of domestic events during her long absence from the official world tour between February 2020 and June 2021. One of them was an appearance in the UK Pro League (an unofficial domestic event), in August 2020. It is instructive to look back on an inter-view she gave to the tournament's website at the time, assessing her future aims: 'My long-term goals in tennis are to be top ten in the world and win Slams – they're my ultimate dreams and I definitely think I have the mentality to do it,' she said. 'I'm pretty ambitious. It's just if my game can follow, but I think with the progress that I'm making at the moment that isn't too far out of the question. I really do believe I can do it. I think I've still got at least fifteen years in the sport, but I would want to be peaking in my twenties, when I'm about twenty-three.'

That week in Sunderland in February 2020 turned out to be a relatively good one for Raducanu, who stayed in a bed and breakfast on the windswept seafront. Despite being in the first year of A-levels, she reached the final, losing to the far more experienced Viktoriya Tomova. The Bulgarian was to go on and carve a little piece of tennis history for herself in the summer of 2020: in the initial WTA (Women's Tennis Association) Tour event to take place after the pandemic hiatus, at the end of July in Sicily, she became the first player to be pulled out of a draw after testing positive for Covid.

Britain's Jack Draper went one better than Raducanu in Sunderland, winning the men's event. He was to play a tournament in South Africa a few weeks later which had the rare distinction of being simply abandoned halfway through, as players scrambled to get back to their home countries. He too would make a breakthrough during the brief grass-court season of 2021, reaching the last eight of the Cinch Championships at London's Queen's Club.

As for his fellow bright British prospect, after February 2020 she would not be seen again at an official world-ranking tournament for more than fifteen months. The pandemic was the biggest reason of all why, before she burst forth at Wimbledon and the US Open, so few people outside the game's parish knew who she was.

There are virtually no recent parallels, with the nearest approximation in previous years being Poland's Iga Świątek winning the 2020 French Open aged nineteen, when ranked 54. Świątek was someone who had taken her school studies seriously into her late teens, something else she had in common with Raducanu. Yet even then, when she won at Roland Garros she had entered that event having played 135 official professional singles matches, including making the fourth round in Paris the previous year. When the British player went into the 2021 US Open, she had played, by comparison, just 86 matches in the pros. The player she beat in the final, nineteen-year-old Leylah Fernandez, had played 161.

Something else notable happened on that otherwise unremarkable day in Sunderland. At lunchtime it emerged that former world No. 1 Maria Sharapova, whose career had subsequently become mired in a drugs-related controversy and suspension, had appeared in *Vogue* magazine announcing that she was quitting tennis. It helps that the magazine's editor-in-chief, Anna Wintour, is one of the sport's highest-profile fans, but very few athletes get the kind of crossover that allows them to pen their retirement letter in such a prestigious publication. Since winning Wimbledon at seventeen in 2004, the Russian had moved beyond the boundaries of tennis and earned that status through her combination of talent, looks and notoriety.

It would not be long before Raducanu featured in the same

pages, following Wimbledon's 2021 Championships. Her post-SW19 appearance in *Vogue* symbolised a rise from obscurity that had taken place with breakneck speed. By virtue of making the fourth round, and her dramatic exit with breathing difficulties, Emma Raducanu was already one of the most recognisable names in British sport. More astonishing, however, was that we had not seen anything yet.

The Bromley girl displays her early promise in Auray in Brittany in 2014 in one of Tennis Europe's leading Under-12 competitions.

2

THE BROMLEY EFFECT

By the early 1990s, prior to the emergence of Tim Henman, Britain had become almost the land that tennis forgot. Wimbledon endured, but the Grand Slams would come and go with the Union Jack being lowered after just a couple of days, despite it being the nation that hosted the world's premier tournament.

One of the few connections that the UK had with the elite end of the sport was Tony Pickard, the former Davis Cup player who had gone on to become the long-serving coach of Stefan Edberg, the men's world No. 1. During one of the regular inquests into the dire state of the British game Pickard, whose views were often sought by the media, ventured that Britain's next Grand Slam champion would probably grow up within a ten-minute walk of an indoor tennis centre.

His comment was prophetic. As it turned out, it certainly did Andy Murray no harm that, in terms of his sporting development, he was raised in Dunblane, a few miles away from the impressive facility at Stirling. When it came to the player who followed Murray in winning a singles Major, a high-class indoor hub had actually been built within the grounds of her school. It could hardly have been better for Emma Raducanu that Bromley Tennis Centre – opened in 2003 at a cost of £2 million – was adjacent to Newstead Wood, the selective grammar school where she had secured one of the much-sought-after places. The only child of Ian and Renee, she had wound up in one of the best locations in the country to hone a tennis player.

The Raducanus had taken a circuitous route to arrive in this commuter area on the fringes of south-east London. Ian had been brought up in Bucharest, while Renee had been born in Shenyang, a city in the north-east of China, not far from the Korean border. From different origins, and seeking a better life, they had met in Toronto, where their only daughter was born.

By the middle of the last decade, Ontario had turned into an unlikely hotbed of tennis. Milos Raonic, Murray's victim in the 2016 Wimbledon final, is from there. So is 2019 women's US Open champion Bianca Andreescu, who is of Romanian heritage. And it was also the place where the two finalists in the 2021 edition of Flushing Meadows, Emma and Leylah Fernandez, spent early years. This is not just coincidence. Toronto is home to a large immigrant population, especially from behind the former Iron Curtain, and the history of tennis shows that such concentrations can be a fertile breeding ground for exceptional tennis talent.

While the sport has long had a presence in Eastern Europe, its status in that part of the world was powered by two particular factors. When tennis became a demonstration sport at the 1984 Los Angeles Olympics, tennis federations in the former Soviet sphere began to receive more government funding. The subsequent fall of the Berlin Wall, and the lifting of travel restrictions, made it a very attractive sporting option for talented children with driven parents. That is why we have seen so many top players with at least some Eastern European heritage over the past thirty years, Emma Raducanu being one of the most recent examples.

After her spectacular success of 2021, there was a natural curiosity about how the family had ended up in Kent. The *Daily Mail*'s David Jones and James Franey tracked down Ian Raducanu's mother, Niculina, to her flat in the Romanian capital. Ian had graduated with an engineering degree from Bucharest's Mihai Viteazul National College before emigrating to Toronto, while Renee had found her way to Canada from Shenyang. Yet it appears they had little or no involvement with the tennis community in their adopted city.

When Emma was two they moved on to work in London, Ian as a project manager in finance and Renee in the world of foreign exchange. They settled into a house in a cul-de-sac on the Orpington/Bromley borders – which in 2021 was briefly to become Britain's most famous semi-detached dwelling.

Around the time of Wimbledon, neighbours spoke of the well-liked, hard-working family whose youngest member had suddenly been propelled to fame by reaching the fourth round at SW19. Raducanu was not, however, the first talented female player from the area – in fact, there was someone who in recent times had beaten her to playing on the Centre Court at the All England Club.

That was Naomi Cavaday, a former Bromley High School pupil. In 2008 she was one of the UK's best prospects and had played on the famous lawns in the first round against Venus Williams, giving a creditable account of herself before losing 7–6, 6–1. There were times over Raducanu's summer when the phrase 'Victory has a thousand fathers, but defeat is an orphan' sprang to mind as her rise was being discussed. Many people emerged as having been connected to her success. It was, however, a plain matter of fact that an unusually large number of coaches, hitting partners and fitness experts had worked with her along the way.

Two of them were Cavaday herself and her brother Nick, the latter as part of his progression towards becoming one of the country's most prominent coaches. A couple of regular themes emerge when examining Raducanu's journey. The most persistent is the constant thirst for knowledge and self-improvement exhibited by her and her family when it came to tennis. Another is that there could have been few better parts of the country to grow up for an aspiring player.

Naomi Cavaday was both fascinated and impressed by what she found in the Raducanus: 'I think their mentality was "Right, we're doing this as a family. Emma's going to be a professional tennis player. That's what she wants to do. We know she's able to do it based on her ability. Who do we need to help us along the way?" It's a very different mentality to almost everybody else in this country, because most parents will hire a coach and say, "You need to turn this person into a tennis player." All the responsibility is on the coach. But if [the Raducanus] felt like they needed something better, they would absolutely go and get it.'

Before concentrating purely on tennis, they ensured that their only child sampled plenty of different sports and activities. Ballet classes were one thing, while there were also regular trips to a converted bus garage in Streatham where she enjoyed go-karting, before graduating to motocross on two wheels. Her fondness for motor sports, especially Formula One, has stayed with her into adulthood.

Yet tennis became her overriding passion. She had first picked up a racket aged five when her parents gave the sport a try in local parks, and she was soon playing at the Parklangley Club and at Bromley Tennis Centre. The first time she got her name on an honours board was when winning the latter's tournament for Under-8s at the age of six. By the age of seven she had made the final of a national winter tournament in Oxfordshire.

One of the first to come across the fledgling talent of Emma Raducanu was Simon Dahdi, who worked for the Lawn Tennis Association as a talent performance coordinator for the southeast and Kent region. He was later to change profession and become a train driver, but a major part of his former job was scouting the best young players.

He first saw her playing at the National Tennis Centre in Roehampton. As is common with the youngest age groups, the competition was being held using less pressurised balls that are easier to hit for children, the idea being that these aid stroke development.

'The top Under-9 players in that age group were playing a mini orange competition with a softer ball. She was in a round-robin group and then had to qualify from there,' he recalls. 'I was watching her for every game because of my position. We had a few players there and she was about the youngest in the whole event.

'[Her father] Ian was sending her over to me between matches for some tips on what had been happening, so we were discussing what was working well and what maybe she could do a little bit better. Match after match she just managed to get through, and she went all the way to the final. It surprised a lot of people at that time.'

Dahdi hailed from the same corner of the country and, like Cavaday, believes that coming from those parts can only have helped.

'Parklangley was one of the top clubs around in the south-east, so they had a number of good young players coming through their programme, with good coaches and good facilities set up for performance players,' he points out. 'She was obviously one of the star young players in the club, but there was a whole group of talented youngsters there as well.

'We've got so many clubs in the area. You travel five minutes in any direction and you've got a club, and a lot of them have indoor courts. I lived in Cornwall for four years and it's completely different down there. You've got to travel to get games and practice and you'll tend to see the same players again and again, which makes it much more difficult to get good. In an area like north Kent you've got a lot of good players within a small radius, good facilities and this large pool of strong opponents. For Emma, Bromley was perfect because she could just walk over to the tennis centre from school.

'She had the whole package, really. She was quiet, very focused and a determined young athlete, listening all the time. She just hung on to every word, the eye contact was there. She could pick up information so well and then was able to apply that into what she was doing with her tennis. The way she was striking the ball was naturally very clean and smooth, like she is now. She was a fantastic mover, her coordination was great. Her concentration levels were very high. She had the technique as well. The serve was a strongly coordinated motion, although that was the one thing which stood out as what she needed to work on. Most things were there.

'My relationship with the parents was really good and we are still friendly. They were very supportive, taking her round competitions and camps. I couldn't fault them.'

Dahdi also believes that her natural intelligence was a big advantage for her tennis, as was the fact that she had retained a wide variety of interests.

'I think you do get children that burn out a little bit. They focus too much on one sport and they can lose that love for it. Doing other activities is brilliant, in my opinion. I remember the time I was in a meeting with other coaches when we found out that she was doing motocross, and we all laughed a little bit, and it was like, "Okay, that's fine." You want to keep them happy and keep them motivated.

'Newstead Wood is a difficult school to get into and it helps to be intelligent in tennis because a lot of it is about problem-solving at speed: to work out how you need to compete against your opponent, what sort of tactics to use, what works and what doesn't. You could always see with Emma from a young age, all the way to when she was playing at the US Open, she has that problem-solving ability.'

Dahdi also points out that working with several different coaches was nothing out of the ordinary.

'She moved over to Bromley Tennis Centre when she was ten. She started doing some work with Nick Cavaday and spent time with Andrew Richardson as well. Then she moved on to Alastair Filmer for at least a couple of years, up to the age of about 13. [Clint Harris, a locally based New Zealander, was another who became involved.] It's actually quite a rare thing to work with the same coach for a lot of years. If there were different coaches involved with her, it was partly because other coaches moved on themselves. Nick went working on the tour, Andrew moved to Suffolk. After a few years Alastair moved on. It's just what can happen.'

Naomi Cavaday had two spells playing on the WTA Tour, a life which she admits could be highly stressful at times. She also did some coaching, and it was not long before Raducanu was on her radar.

'When I was playing on the circuit I'd often be at Bromley and I knew all the coaches there. I'd ask who are the standouts? In one of the first conversations I had, I remember it was just all about Emma.'

Like many young players, she was brought up progressing from one different ball colour to another.

'She was playing green-ball tennis and it was obvious she was very good,' says Cavaday. 'Green-ball is something that can be difficult, because when children are younger, and playing with the red or orange, the pressure of the ball and the size of the court are relative to your height and your abilities. When you progress to green you have a full-size court, but it's a soft, dead ball. You can actually get away with hacking and playing some horrible shots, but that didn't work against Emma because her movement was so good.

'You'd see some youngsters really struggling with the bounce. She had the strength to hit quality shots like she was playing full-on proper tennis, which I thought was interesting. Every couple of years you do see somebody like that coming through and she was already in that category. At that stage I'd been in tennis for ten years and I'd maybe seen four or five players like that.

'She moved over to working with [my brother] Nick and that was after working with Andrew Richardson. Straight off the bat, I was always talking to Nick about her. I think a big feature to me at that time was her energy just walking to the court. She was always walking in with such positivity. These really young kids who have signed up to a programme, they are playing sometimes more than once a day. There's a lot going on in their life and you have days when they just sort of drag their bag to the courts. But she would always bop in with a little skip, and you knew she wanted to be there.'

That ability and enthusiasm, coupled with the expertise of coaches like Filmer, was a potent combination. Around the same time Raducanu also made an impression on former British No. 1 Anne Keothavong, who would go on to become her captain in the Billie Jean King Cup (formerly the Fed Cup) and an influential figure at the All England Club.

'Soon after I retired in 2013 I was doing my coaching qualifications at the LTA and on a couple of sessions I was given Emma and Indy Spink, another girl who was good, as my guinea pigs,' she recalls. 'I had been told Emma was promising and it was pretty obvious why. You don't see many kids trying to take the ball early and on the rise like she was doing. I wasn't long off the tour and I remember thinking "I'm really having to concentrate here" when I was hitting with her. You could see how keen she was to learn.'

Cavaday, however, was a more regular sparring partner through their Kent connection: 'I was a local girl and I suppose I turned into a bit of a player-mentor. She started getting more serious about tennis and when she got to about thirteen, people were saying that no one had played like that since Laura Robson. I was around her family and was asked to hit with her a few times a week. That was the sort of time when I stopped competing professionally and as soon as they heard that, they asked me to come and do some sessions. I was living up near Watford, so it was quite a drive.

'I'd go down there every Monday night and stay with my parents so I could do some stuff with her before school. I think she was missing the first lesson and I would do two or three tennis sessions with her early in the week. I could have been coaching somewhere more convenient, to tell the truth, but I wanted to do it because I liked her and her family, and their attitude impressed me.

'They would always ask questions. They respected what I'd achieved, but they made no bones about the fact that they wanted her to be better than I was, which is fair enough. You just don't get that kind of curiosity or drive from most young British players, which can be a bit surprising and disappointing.

'Ian [Raducanu] has incredibly high standards. He's very softly spoken and respectful. It's always a two-way conversation with him. He is very interested in people, it doesn't matter who you are. He would always ask a lot of questions because he looks for that extra depth in a subject. He would say, "Oh, wait a minute, can you fully explain that?" He wanted to understand tennis and absorb because he hadn't played himself.

'There are people who've commented on the way that they've moved from one coach to the other, but I think it's because Ian feels like everybody's got something to offer. There's always something that you can learn from somebody.

'Whenever Renee was around, we'd have nice conversations and she was pleasant to deal with. They're very similar. She's very switched on. She would sometimes ask me my opinion on coaches. I'd start trying to be diplomatic about certain things and she'd just say, "No, I want your honest opinion, I don't want the diplomatic stuff. I want you to tell me what you actually think about this person, and then we'll make our decision after that."'

* * *

Cavaday's involvement waned as Raducanu's game evolved to the point where she was starting to travel overseas. The Kent schoolgirl became more involved with the Lawn Tennis Association programmes, with her potential becoming more obvious. Before long she was starting to collect trophies.

Late in 2011 she won her first **Under-9 winter national** event staged by the LTA, at the Graves Tennis Centre in Yorkshire. The following April she travelled to **Bressuire** in western France to win a first Under-11 title against international opposition at an event run by Tennis Europe. She moved on from Bickley Primary School after gaining a prized place at Newstead Wood, whose motto is 'Fortitudine Crescamus' – May We Grow In Strength. It is somewhere with a record of developing high-achieving young people, such as Olympic sprinter Dina Asher-Smith.

Clearly the tennis was becoming more serious, requiring a juggling act with her studies. The commitment of ferrying her to and from training and tournaments is something any parent can identify with. More titles around the Kent area were banked, but increasingly she was making her mark much further afield. By 2014 she had won another European tournament in the Portuguese city of **Braga**. This was followed by selection for the LTA team representing Great Britain at the Under-12 **European Winter Cup** in London, playing alongside two of her national rivals, Lillian Mould and Indy Spink. They lost to the eventual champions, representing the Czech Republic, but defeated Italy to come third. Raducanu was victorious in ten of the twelve matches she played.

Later in 2014 she would enter the prestigious Under-12 **Orange Bowl** in Miami, where she lost in the first round but won the consolation event.

Cavaday, who has become one of the more perceptive commentators in the media about the British game, never doubted that Raducanu was on the road to becoming something special. Yet of course, like everyone else, she never imagined she had been hitting with someone who would become US Open champion at the age of eighteen.

'I was surprised at the speed of it, obviously, but not surprised it actually happened at some point. I'd had lots of conversations with my brother about Emma – we always felt like she was a guarantee for the top fifty. We were pretty confident she was going to do incredibly well, but players can struggle for all sorts of reasons. There is a lot that can go wrong. But that real self-belief, you can't fake it up at the top level. Once she really believed she could belong at the top, there would be no ceiling. It would be top twenty, top ten, and then you never know.

'I had thought that if everything fell into place with me, and I had made all the right decisions and had some luck with draws, I could have been a top-fifty player. If you look at the career of Jo Konta, it took her some time to get things right. Then she moved to work with [Spanish coach] Esteban Carril and he was the right fit, and then off she goes. With Emma I thought that even if they didn't make the right decisions, she would still make the top at some point.'

In a hugely competitive individual sport, where opponents are drawn from all around the world, there is much to navigate. And while tennis is not an expensive sport to play recreationally, as sometimes imagined, becoming an elite player most definitely involves some hefty costs.

That is where an organisation like Tennis First can help. Run by former British player and senior Wimbledon figure Ken Weatherley, it is a charity which seeks to provide support to the families of youngsters who are thinking of having a shot at the elite level. It is not just about finance, but about providing advice on the complexities of the journey. When Raducanu made her first breakthroughs at senior level she became the seventeenth British player it had helped make it into the target zone of the world's top 250. Other alumni have included the likes of Kyle Edmund, Jack Draper and Anne Keothavong.

Again, the theme of the Raducanus' desire for knowledge shines through: 'I always try to speak to the parents of prospective grantees,' says Weatherley. 'Ian did not have a tennis background, but he was always inquisitive and keen to glean information both technical and about the pathway to becoming a pro. That is a complicated area and requires a lot of decisions to be made. There are pushy parents who can be a pain in the neck, but he was not one of those. He was always very nice and motivated by what was best for his daughter.

'Another aspect is that he would not be swayed by orthodox thinking on coaching. I would say he does not suffer fools gladly. For us the idea is that we give them some support so that they have the chance to fulfil that potential and then, as with Emma, we would stop when they are getting sufficient help from elsewhere.'

In November 2021 Raducanu – by now besieged with requests for her time – was declining almost every invitation to attend functions. Yet she showed her appreciation for that initial backing from Tennis First by turning up, in the middle of her off-season training block, as the star turn at their annual fundraising event.

'A lot of the time when I was younger any bit of funding I received was so beneficial and useful, so they really helped me out and I'm happy to be here tonight,' she told the black-tie audience at the All England Club.

Weatherley also points out that the social demographic of those trying to have a crack at the top level is much more diverse than some preconceptions of tennis in the UK, and that Raducanu may further accelerate that: 'I think there is a cultural element involved. In tennis it usually takes a lot of commitment from at least one parent, and there is often a different drive and ambition in families who have arrived here from elsewhere for children to achieve their maximum potential. In tennis there has definitely been a significant shift towards kids who are first- or second-generation Brits, more ethnic minorities, and that is a really positive thing.'

His organisation had done its bit in helping her along the way in the early days. Before long it became increasingly clear just how far the journey might take her.

Taking a break from schoolwork in 2017 to play in the junior tournament at Wimbledon for the first time – here facing Taipei's En Shuo Liang.

3

A-LEVELS AND AIR MILES

As Emma Raducanu burst into the public consciousness during the summer of 2021, her one-time coach Matt James looked at the reaction and afforded himself a wry smile.

'The impression most people had was that she had come from nowhere, and of course I completely understand that is how you would see it if you had only a casual interest,' he says. 'But anyone involved with the British game would know that this wasn't the case.'

Given that there are no overnight fairy tales in tennis, it is difficult to argue with that.

James had been brought in by the Lawn Tennis Association in late summer 2018 to work with a player who, by then, was already starting to fulfil the expectations placed upon her.

For more than three years she had been making regular visits to Roehampton's National Tennis Centre to participate in LTA national training camps for her age group. These were an established part of her life by 2015, which was also the year she made her first ever appearance on the grass courts a couple of miles along the road, at the All England Club. The twelve-year-old had made it through the south-east regional qualifiers of the HSBC Road To Wimbledon, an event designed to give British youngsters their first taste of the grass at SW19.

It was a fun few days yet, as ever, the benchmark for success in tennis is seen in international terms. Soon it was time to try and take the first step on the ladder of the official junior world rankings. And so it was that in November 2015, the young Raducanu took a trip up to **Liverpool**. That is, naturally, a city synonymous with a different sport, although it is also the place that has recently produced two of Britain's most acclaimed doubles players, Neal and Ken Skupski. It is also where Norwegian promoter Anders Borg has worked hard to maintain a tennis presence amid the mania for football, staging a winter event for juniors and a professional exhibition tournament in the summer during the pre-Wimbledon weeks.

His Nike Junior International is held in the suburb of Wavertree, and this edition was due to begin three days after Raducanu turned thirteen, the age when you are allowed to compete in such events. This was designated Grade 5, the lowest rung of the global junior ladder run by the ITF (International Tennis Federation), but it is a well-known fixture on the circuit. It can also boast an impressive honour roll of past winners. Novak Djokovic, Caroline Wozniacki and Eugenie Bouchard are among those to have held the trophy in the past before going on to greater things. And by the time the week was out it had another one to add to that list: Emma Raducanu. Despite being the youngest competitor, she won five matches and in the final beat fellow Brit Lauryn John-Baptiste – more than three years her senior – 6–1, 6–4.

This drew the attention of the insiders who follow such results, although in the history of female junior tennis it still did not compare to some other feats. Martina Hingis, for instance, won the 1994 French Open girls' event when she was just twelve. Yet when looking at Raducanu's fledgling career, it has to be recognised that this is a different era. Amid concerns that young girls were being driven too hard, various regulations (quickly dubbed the Capriati Rules after the former American prodigy's struggles) had been established, limiting the amount of senior competitive tennis that could be played during adolescence. That is one reason why we see fewer high-profile wunderkinds these days, and the sport is probably healthier for that.

Raducanu, beavering away at school, was in no hurry to capitalise on Liverpool. She did not play another official junior worldranking tournament for nearly eight months, until July 2016, and then only played three that whole year. She rounded off 2016 with another trip to the **Orange Bowl** in Florida, this time playing in the Under-14s, in which she came third, much improved from her previous visit.

There was more steady progress in 2017, although by historical standards it was again relatively unspectacular. She worked on her tennis at Bromley and Roehampton while gradually stepping up her international schedule. After winning Grade 4 events in **Oslo** and **Hamburg**, the summer saw her picked, at just fourteen, for the annual GB v USA **Maureen Connolly Cup**, featuring the respective nations' top Under-18 players, held that year at Southsea in Portsmouth. She won one of her two matches there and a few days later made her debut at **junior Wimbledon**. That ended with a narrow second-round defeat to Taipei's En Shuo Liang. Arguably more of a highlight was her managing to secure a selfie with a passing Roger Federer.

One of the reasons Raducanu's junior career did not attract vast attention was that she was never to progress beyond the last eight at the junior Slams, and in some ways that may have been a blessing in disguise. Laura Robson had won the Wimbledon girls' event at fourteen, and from then on it always seemed questionable whether that success, and the pressures it brought, could be considered helpful in the long run.

Raducanu's outing at Wimbledon in 2017 was to be her last junior ranking event of the season. So far, so reasonably good, but 2018 would be the year of lift-off. Now fifteen, this was when she would start travelling in earnest, the point at which the business of trying to become an elite player brings with it significant bills to pay. The LTA was, by this point, giving her considerable funding support.

As the governing body's head of women's tennis, Iain Bates has sat in on dozens of meetings where the level of financial help to individuals is discussed and a number of criteria are taken into consideration. The Raducanus, for example, had planned to begin the year with a couple of Grade 3 ITF junior events in India, which would involve considerable outlay.

'When we are asked for funding, we look at questions like what's the coaching set-up? Are there any wider sports-medicine requirements? What's the tournament schedule? We have a pot of money based on the player's potential and we work with them,' says Bates. 'We allocate pockets of money to make sure the players get what they need. Those events in India and the other ones earlier that year, Emma would be tackling them herself because it was the right schedule for her. I've been asked quite a lot when I first became aware of Emma, but I honestly can't remember, because she was just one of those whose name was always mentioned in a very positive way going back a long time.

'She didn't play much in the way of juniors beyond the age of sixteen, which is the most simple explanation why she didn't achieve more at the Slams. There were a couple of summers where she had done her school exams and then literally gone straight onto the grass. It also shows the strength of the junior Slams on the girls' side. A few of those players who beat her [in the junior Slams] have rolled on to play the very highest level of tennis. At certain stages a player will develop quicker and then stall, but the main thing is to be on the right overall trajectory. When the decision was made to promote her to the full Pro Scholarship Programme level [the summer of 2018] she was the youngest to receive that since it had been running. I think the reason it had taken its own time was that she was focusing on academics largely, then she had that great start to the year in India and it took off from there.'

In January 2018 she had headed for the cool of the northern subcontinent winter with her mother and won back-to-back events – in **Chandigarh**, followed by **New Delhi** – dropping only one set. Coincidentally, it was an almost identical mini-circuit to the one Tim Henman and Andrew Richardson, two people who were part of her New York triumph, had travelled on as they cut their teeth together more than twenty years previously. The roll continued the following month when, accompanied by father Ian, she went to **Chişinău** in Moldova and won her first Grade 2. Then it was on to **Lithuania**, this time with Jane O'Donoghue from the LTA, who was overseeing her progress and became a key confidante and component in her progress. Roman Kelečić, the coach who had been working with her at Bromley, was also there, and yet again she won the tournament.

These twenty consecutive wins led to the conclusion that it was time, finally, to try a first professional event with full world ranking points at stake. So, in the school Easter holidays, she went off to the western Chinese city of **Nanjing** to play two tournaments offering $15,000 in prize money, the very lowest on the circuit. On Saturday, 24 March 2018, Raducanu played her first pro match, defeating unranked twenty-one-year-old Japanese player Satsuki Koike 6–0, 6–0. The field consisted mainly of Chinese players and she was to fall to one of them, Siqi Cao, in the third and final qualifying round. The following week, at the same venue, she came through qualifying and then made the quarter-final before losing to seventh seed Xiaodi You. Fatigued, she retired after a first-set tiebreak, having played five matches to get there.

In mid-May 2018, while the world's attention was focusing on the marriage of the Duke and Duchess of Sussex, Raducanu was busy winning what would be her first professional title. She had travelled with her father to **Tiberias** in Israel, by the shores of Lake Galilee, to play another $15,000 event. Faced with a more international field of hopefuls – and temperatures that hit 45 degrees – she needed to win just one qualifying match to make the main draw. She then proceeded to win each match in straight sets and, on the day of the royal wedding, saw off Belgium's Hélène Scholsen 7–5, 6–4 to take the title. That was enough to earn her a first world ranking of 885. At 15, she had become the youngest player that year, from anywhere, to make a Futures final.

Returning to the mix of school and tennis, she travelled to Paris in June 2018 to make what would be her only appearance in the **French Open juniors**. Scuffling on an outside court besides the tree-lined Boulevard d'Auteuil, she lost in the second round to the highly rated Clara Tauson. The Dane was someone she would repeatedly run into – and usually lose against – in her early career. An appearance at an ITF professional event in **Manchester**, on the grass swing that followed the clay, then saw her lose in three sets to Harriet Dart, a more experienced GB player. Yet by the time Wimbledon arrived there was definitely more of a buzz around the fifteen-year-old from Kent, who was starting to achieve things rarely seen from a British youngster.

She made her debut in main **Wimbledon qualifying** at the end of June, the preliminary event which grants survivors entry to the main event. That resulted in a first-round loss to Czech Barbora Stefkova in three sets. This early-summer mini-run of defeats, however, did little to dampen interest in her when the junior Wimbledon event began in the tournament's second week. By now she was very much on the radar of the major management companies in tennis, most of whom were vying for her signature as an unusual prospect. That she was representing a significant commercial tennis market such as Great Britain only upped the interest.

Different agencies were making presentations to the Raducanus as part of the elaborate courtship process that accompanies the pursuit of teenagers reckoned to have real potential. Closely tracking her for more than a year had been John Morris, then working for IMG. One of Morris's occupations was the demanding task of looking after the Australian Nick Kyrgios, but as an experienced talent scout for the agency he had long been convinced of Raducanu's ability.

Morris had an idea involving another of IMG's clients, Li Na, who had become China's first tennis superstar by winning the US and Australian Opens, before retiring in 2014. She had been a childhood idol of the young GB player. 'Li Na was at Wimbledon doing some promotional work and I saw her up at the house in the village that Nick [Kyrgios] had been staying at but vacated by then,' recalls Morris. 'I asked if she could come and have a look at Emma, who was playing Leylah Fernandez in the second round [of junior Wimbledon], and slightly to my amazement she was happy to pop by. She watched some of the match and both she and her husband were impressed by what they saw. I think Emma noticed them watching and it was quite something for her.

'Everyone was trying to sign Emma and I had been talking to Ian. He was more interested in information and what we thought in terms of coaching options than he was about money. I recall that he was very focused on making sure that Emma had coaching that was specific to her age and her level at that time. My coaching background perhaps helped because I was able to come up with a list of names who met those criteria. From day one he would say that he was not an expert in coaching or training or marketing, but that he did have a lot of experience of being a project manager, and that he would be managing the project.'

Later in the year, that autumn, IMG would win the competition for her signature. Her affairs would subsequently come to be handled by Max Eisenbud, one of the sport's best-known agents, who had looked after Maria Sharapova and Li Na, among others.

On the court, nobody present for the second-round match between Raducanu and Fernandez on 10 July 2018 would have been aware of their meeting's future significance. On Court 17, the last of the row of four sandwiched between Wimbledon's Centre and Number One, there were plenty of seats available for the match between two players with strong ties to Toronto.

The result was a 6–2, 6–4 victory for the British player, sealed with a driven cross-court backhand. She went on to make the quarter-finals, in which she lost heavily to Poland's Iga Świątek, who two years later would become the French Open champion.

Among the spectators for both matches was Iain Bates: 'You watch so many matches over the course of a year and there was nothing truly exceptional about that one against Leylah, although it was a very high-level contest between two junior players,' he said. 'You wouldn't have thought that in three years they're going to play each other in a Grand Slam final, but you knew they were both going to be very good. Emma then played Świątek, and you have to remember that by then, as with Tauson at the French, Iga was already being identified as an outstanding prospect, so the result was not that surprising.'

If any player has tried to make it to the elite end of tennis, then the chances are high that they will have ventured to the Kaya Belek tennis resort in the southern coastal city of Antalya in Turkey. They may well have experienced the Egyptian holiday spot of Sharm El Sheikh, too. Both are prolific hosts of Futures events that offer an early chance of advancement to aspiring players, and are not just one-off weeks, like Sunderland. Their business plan is quite simple: they host on-site tournaments year round to keep their hotels busy with a constant churn of guests who are mining the valuable currency of world ranking points. In normal times they would host at least thirty such tournaments per year.

And so it was that Emma Raducanu found herself in this part of the Mediterranean in late October 2018, seeking to build on the gains from earlier in the season. She was now armed with a full scholarship from the LTA worth around £80,000 annually, and her support set-up had been adjusted as she looked to scale the bottom layers of the professional pyramid. Travelling with her was Matt James, with whom she had begun hitting on the grass during the summer. By then Nigel Sears was being employed as a consultant to oversee the career of Raducanu and, at his instigation, James had been signed up by the LTA to work specifically with this schoolgirl from Kent.

Sears had become one of Britain's most seasoned coaches, having worked at the very top end of the game with the likes of Ana Ivanovic, Daniela Hantuchová and latterly Anett Kontaveit of Estonia. He was at least as well known for being the father-in-law of Andy Murray, since the big star of the British game's marriage to his daughter Kim. Few knew more about what it would take to reach the highest levels than Sears, and he had been impressed by James's work as an occasional hitter for some of his star clients. The head coach on the tennis programme at Millfield School in Somerset, James was persuaded to switch to the LTA and help develop one of the country's outstanding prospects as she entered its highest-level scholarship programme.

Having done some initial work, post-Wimbledon, with Sears down at his base near Brighton, Raducanu headed to New York, for the **US Open juniors** in September 2018. For the only time prior to her historic feat of 2021, she was to experience the unique hustle and bustle of Flushing Meadows, where the phrase 'Quiet, please' may as well be uttered in some distant foreign tongue. Again, it was a strong if not spectacular performance in the mini-Grand Slam. She made the quarter-finals, but then managed to win only two games against French player Clara Burel, who was soon to become the world's highest-ranked junior.

After the previous round before that match, the British player had been brought in to one of the small breakout areas in the press room for a post-match interview, more intimate than the main room she would be occupying three years later, and a small handful of reporters listened in. She had become the first British junior woman to make the last eight of two straight junior Slams since Annabel Croft in 1984. Yet her abrupt departure at the hands of Burel at the last-eight stage meant that any media exposure was minimal.

In the juniors a law of diminishing returns sometimes applies when it comes to a player's development. Some will reach the point where playing at that level is of limited further value, and with that in mind, it was decided that James would start travelling with her on the full professional tour. The technical standard among the pros is higher, and the physical side more demanding. Not only that, but it is also a less friendly environment than being among friends more easily made amid the innocence of the junior circuit. The first stop was a $25,000 event in **Lisbon**, where she lost in the second round of qualifying. The next month, October, she journeyed along the well-trodden path to **Antalya** – and went straight through the field at the $15,000 event, winning each match in straight sets to take the title.

'Lisbon was a difficult one. It was a bit of an eye-opener, a reality check that although people were talking about her, she was not a superstar yet,' recalls James. 'She was quite tired after New York and in hindsight, she probably shouldn't have gone to that tournament in Portugal. We had done some hard sessions down in Brighton after America and she did not have much in her legs. Antalya is a bit like Sharm El Sheikh: it's a resort and it's easy to manage because everything is in the same place. But the courts were pretty poor. There were cracks in them and it was more like a local club really.

'You're starting off in the Futures, looking for points to go up in the world rankings, and it's the sort of place you travel to because you know you're going to get into the tournament and you're guaranteed hotel rooms and practice. There's a lot of people there that are just starting the journey and ideally you want to get through this stage as quickly as possible. Emma's level was better than everyone, but there is still pressure. The big points are very much loaded towards getting to the semis and finals and that adds to it.

'Physically, she was in a better place by Turkey. We'd had a few weeks to get ready for it and for the player–coach relationship to develop, so it was a lot easier for me to get messages across, and you've got more evidence to base your advice on. In Portugal, tactically she wasn't great, but then there's the mentality. It's interesting to me that even at that level, when it gets a bit close you can already tell that the girls who are low-ranked are not as good under pressure as those ranked higher than them. That's probably one of the things that stood out for me early on – when it got close, Emma was fine under pressure. She actually thrived on it and other girls often hid away, which is why they were stuck in those events.

'I think she was three-love down in the second round and there was some pressure, but she didn't panic. What's really important is when you play your "6 out of 10" tennis you can still get over the line, because you are rarely going to be playing to your ultimate standard.' Still shy of her sixteenth birthday, Raducanu had now collected a second professional title, following her first in Tiberias in May.

A week later they found themselves in the contrasting environment of the **Wirral** on Merseyside for a $25,000 event with a considerably stronger field. The indoor centre at Bidston stands on the edge of a retail park by the side of the M53 that leads to the Mersey tunnel, not in one of the leafier parts of the peninsula that protrudes between Liverpool and north Wales. Eschewing the official hotel, they chose to stay across the river in the city centre down by the water.

'She doesn't really fuss too much about being around other players and it's all business when it comes to the tournament. It was very much kind of keeping ourselves to ourselves to really work,' says James. 'It was a weird kind of week because beforehand she was complaining of pain in her shin and the physios weren't sure whether she should really even be playing. This is where the mindset comes in. She was like "No, I'm playing this tournament." She quite liked that feeling of proving people wrong a little bit. She said, "It's okay, even if I've got a bit of pain. I want to go up there and you can watch me go and compete now."'

There were to be a couple of eye-catching wins as she reached the semi-finals. In the second round she faced her first ever top-200 opponent in Austria's Barbara Haas, and in the following match defeated Belgium's Greet Minnen, ranked 310 but well on her predicted trajectory to the top 100, which she duly achieved.

'The Haas one was interesting because Emma's movement was unbelievable, it really shone through,' says James, who is blessed with an encyclopaedic memory of tennis matches. 'The opponent was a good counter-puncher, but Emma could hit through that sort of player. Barbara took a long medical time-out in the third set and you're worried how Emma might react, but it didn't put her off. In the next match, against Minnen, I had never seen her serve as well. The standard of that match for the level of tournament was outstanding, it was a great contest to watch. Greet's girlfriend Alison [Van Uytvanck, fellow Belgian player] was ranked 60 in the world at the time and she was there just practising and watching. She told me after the match, "This girl is going to be good." That really stuck with me because it was the first time I had heard it from someone from outside the UK who had made it to a high level.'

Raducanu played sparingly for the next five months, during which she turned sixteen. A lot of pre-season work was done, mainly at Bromley, as she focused largely on school work. The only foreign trip in that time was a visit to the **Australian Open** juniors in January 2019. She made the semis of the primary warm-up tournament, where again she lost to Denmark's Clara Tauson. A first-round exit meant she provided precious little distraction from the main event, again slipping beneath the radar.

Upon returning, she was to get her first taste of being around senior team tennis when Bath was the host of a four-cornered edition of the group stages of the Fed Cup (now known as the Billie Jean King Cup). Jo Konta, Heather Watson and Katie Boulter were the bigger names playing for the hosts before a packed crowd, but Raducanu was asked along to be a non-selected part of the squad captained by Anne Keothavong.

Iain Bates had been involved in that decision in his role with the LTA: 'When you have a young player showing the level of potential that she had, it was already evident that at some point in the future she was going to be a key part of the team. This was the first time there was a really logical opportunity to bring her in – I guess primarily to bring her into the fold so she could experience the workings of the squad and its culture. Secondly, she could act as another high-grade sparring partner. She was very good around the group, sort of confident. She had to make a speech to the team before the match, as is tradition, because that was the first time she was part of the group. And then we also made her do another one when she was part of the actual nominated team in Bratislava twelve months later. The speech was a kind of coming together of all her personal attributes, her linguistic skills and humour. Both of the rookie speeches that she did I think highlighted her in a really nice way to the other players. She was fun to be around. We joke that those speeches are now the benchmark for other newcomers.'

This was GCSE year and that, combined with the limits on how many pro events she could play, meant that her schedule continued to be highly selective. By the summer of 2019 she had only played two more world-ranking events, with a return to the Tour in late March in the form of a trip to Israel in the Easter holidays. She scrapped her way to the final in **Tel Aviv**, losing to the much more experienced Italian Corinna Dentoni, and that was to be followed immediately by a slightly more competitive indoor ITF event in **Bolton**, where she was to record her most notable win to date.

'It was very windy in Israel, which kind of evens things out and you've got to battle with things like the ball-toss on serve,' says James. 'You couldn't recreate that sort of stuff in practice, so it was really valuable and another learning experience. She lost the final and had checked out a little bit, wanting to get out of there. Her leg was hurting and her dad didn't really want her to play Bolton. We got checked with a physio, literally stopping over in the National Tennis Centre for one night, and then went straight up to Lancashire.'

In the quarter-final she faced Spain's Paula Badosa, a top-ten star of the future who was to win the prestigious Indian Wells event in October 2021. She was already ranked 130, the highest-calibre opponent Raducanu had faced, but the younger player proceeded to hammer her 6–1, 6–2.

'I thought of that Badosa match when I was watching Emma at the US Open [in 2021], because everything was just clicking in the same way,' says James. 'Badosa was serving wide to her forehand and Emma was rifling it back. Badosa's own forehand wasn't really a weapon back then and she was counter-punching from the back, but Emma was so loose and hitting through her. I thought, "Wow, she can really compete at this high level, especially against the counter-punchers." She played [fellow Brit] Jodie Burrage in the next round, who is a friend and one of her peer group, which makes it a bit different. In truth she could have won the match, but Jodie served well in the third set and got through it.

'After that tournament the studies completely took over. At times she was just playing once or twice a week in the busy times of her GCSE exams. It was tough to get her on court because she was so focused on doing well in them. I think she felt she was very much behind in the studying and that she had to do more than everyone else. She reckoned that if she wanted to get good results, she was going to have to do ten hours of academic work every day. That's Emma – she gets into the zone when she wants to achieve something, and this was just in a different area to tennis.' The hard work paid off again as her GCSEs yielded excellent results. Taking Maths, Further Maths, English Language and Literature, French and all the sciences, she returned high-grade Nines interspersed with three Eights.

Once more, Raducanu's results on grass suffered through the lack of preceding time on court and, two years before she blasted through to Wimbledon's fourth round in 2021, she sank – again – without much trace during the highest-profile period of the British tennis year. She lost in the first round of the **Wimbledon main event's qualifying** to Taipei's En Shuo Liang. When it came to the **juniors** she was ousted, albeit narrowly, in the first round by the relatively unheralded Polish player Martyna Kubka. That was to be not just her last appearance at SW19 before the big breakthrough of

2021, but the last time she played a junior tournament of any description.

There was not much sign of any undue hurry to make up lost ground as she did not play a ranking event until September 2019 at **Roehampton**. 'It was a bit of a shame that she couldn't put her level on court over that grass swing, and you had to accept that it was going to take more time to get through that phase of $25,000 tournaments,' says James. 'She also went to China for a couple of weeks to see family that summer, so didn't come back to play events until the early autumn. She did fine in them, but at the time she was often battling with niggles in her body [a sore wrist had been among them]. We were in a cycle where she'd play a tournament a little undercooked, do quite well because she was already a very good player, but then need some more time off.'

By now she was also doing some work with Belgian coach Philippe Dehaes at the National Tennis Centre in Roehampton. Mainly through his work with Russian Daria Kasatkina and Australian Daria Gavrilova, he had acquired a particular reputation for helping players transition their games to be more equipped for the high levels of the professional tour. He identified that a change was needed to the Raducanu forehand, and so worked on getting her to alter her grip on the shot, imparting a little less topspin but gaining some power without losing control. That became a key building block of her technique.

It should be remembered that Raducanu was still only sixteen and was being kept from the tennis hothouse to live a relatively normal life among fellow A-level pupils at Newstead Wood.

Therefore, making the quarters and semis of those back-to-back autumnal events at Roehampton was still a very respectable showing. It was not, however, the stuff of banner headlines.

With a ranking in the mid-500s, it was decided to finish the year with a tournament in **Minsk**, the capital of Belarus, and a pre-Christmas trip to India in the company of other aspiring British players. It would mean more time off school, but by now she was accustomed to doing a lot of her studies remotely via laptop. These were more hard yards, and she 'celebrated' her seventeenth birthday in Belarus by qualifying and then making the quarter-finals of another $25,000 tournament.

'Minsk wasn't great. I just remember it being very cold. We didn't see anything but grey sky the whole time,' says James. 'She didn't really enjoy it. I thought she was going to win that, because she was the best player there, but again she wasn't quite physically ready and couldn't keep it going.'

The trip to India in December took in two $25,000 tournaments, the first in the remote tennis outpost of **Solapur**, followed by another further north in **Pune**. Raducanu was to win the latter after an all-British final against Naiktha Bains.

'We had spoken to a few Indian people and even they were not sure where Solapur was,' recalls James. 'We ended up flying to Hyderabad and then taking a four-hour taxi there. Actually, the hotel turned out to be perfectly good although it was in the middle of nowhere, but Emma got food poisoning and had to retire when playing Katie Boulter in the second round. Nobody else got it. It was just one of those things.'

'Pune is a much bigger city, but when we went there expectations had probably been lowered a little bit. Getting two matches in the qualifying helped, even though they were against a lesser level of opponent. We would do video analysis before every match and that is where we always felt we gained on opponents because we put a lot of work into that. The analyst team back at the LTA put matches online for us, and if no Brit had ever played a particular player we'd be scouting them, just watching and looking for weaknesses. I can recall that, for instance, we had a look at her first-round opponent there, Valeriya Strakhova, and saw that the second serve might be a vulnerability which could be attacked. Then if you got on the front foot in rallies you could use patterns of play that would make her uncomfortable. Emma beat her 6–0, 6–0.

'It really helped on that trip to have quite a few Brits around, players and coaches, because everyone could spend time together in the evenings and support each other in matches. I felt that week was a massive stepping stone because she really had to battle through. I remember the semi-final against [Olga] Doroshina, which went to three long sets, and Emma completely hustled for that one. She wanted me to move from one end of the court to the other to support her and give her encouragement, I had never done that before. She was saying, "Matt you've got to effing help me get through this match." She had nothing left. She really needed grit to get through those matches because it was so hot out there, the balls got slow and it was just a dogfight. Those are the times I'll remember, because it was a huge effort from her.

'It was difficult before the final because over the last few days of the tournament we were having every dinner together with Naiktha and her dad. It was obviously a great feeling that they were both in the final, but it was a real shame that one of them would have to lose. It was a big match for Naiktha as well, because she was going up the rankings at the time. It was the seventh match of the week for Emma and her legs did not have much left, so I hoped she could just stay in the contest and make it close and see what happened. She had the energy to pull off a few winners at important times. The match wasn't great quality, to be honest, and not easy for either of them, but Emma took it 6–4 in a deciding set.

'I left there very encouraged. She very much has her own mind and will go with her own instincts on things. Sometimes when people say "You can't do this" she will really want to prove them wrong. If she listened to everybody else, then she would not have done what she has done. Most of the time she is proved right when she goes with her gut instinct.'

Iain Bates was also on that trip and was similarly impressed: 'It tells you a lot that it was just before Christmas and she really wanted to stick with it to the end. That is again one of those really rare qualities in someone of sixteen. In that situation, there might have been social stuff on at home. You could be very keen to fly back from a trip like that. The fact that she stuck with it speaks volumes for the mentality and the focus she has.'

Now with a world ranking closer to 350, Raducanu could begin 2020 with the ability to get into bigger events (in tennis the entry system into tournaments is done by ranking, which is why that number by your name is so key). It also made her a pick for the Great Britain playing squad that would travel to Bratislava in early February 2020 to take on Slovakia, in a bid to qualify for the World Group in the now renamed Billie Jean King Cup.

Prior to departure she did an interview with *Metro* journalist George Bellshaw. As he recounted on his *Love Tennis Podcast*, he did not think a great deal about it at the time, given her relatively low profile. She told him, 'My parents, they have pretty high expectations, but it's good because it always pushes me to do better. They weren't into sport at all before me, and they just want me to do well in anything I choose to do, so as I've chosen tennis, they are going to push me to be the best and I'm going to push myself. At the beginning I didn't like it at all, I hated tennis, but I gradually fell in love with winning, working hard and seeing the results and hard work pay off.'

In addition to making a lauded debutante's speech in Bratislava, she beat Heather Watson in a practice set during the preparatory days, but was deemed too inexperienced to make the starting line-up, with the much higher-ranked Watson and Harriet Dart preferred.

Her first tournament of the year, a week later in **Glasgow**, ended prematurely when she suffered an acute back spasm and had to be carried off the court by Matt James and her fitness trainer, Gareth Shelbourne. She had to spend the next twenty-four hours in bed back at the hotel, unable to move. It improved over the following days and, back in London, she deemed that she was fit enough to go up to **Sunderland** late in the month for yet another $25,000 event, despite some misgivings among those around her.

That turned out to be a tournament she could have won, but her Bulgarian opponent, the world No. 151 Viktoriya Tomova, edged her out 6–3 in the deciding set of the final. If there was any disappointment, it was tempered by infinitely more significant matters being afoot. The mystery virus from Asia was starting to arrive in Europe and it would stop the world in its tracks. Within weeks James would find himself on furlough, while Raducanu would be locked down at home along with the rest of the country, her career-high ranking of 333 on hold. Everything, for everyone, was about to change.

Urging on partner Kyle Edmund of the 'British Bulldogs' in their mixed-doubles match against Andy Murray and Naomi Broady of the 'Union Jacks' in the Battle of the Brits team tennis event in Roehampton in August 2020.

4

LOCKED DOWN

Europe, the epicentre of the tennis world, had a rude awakening on the Monday morning of 9 March 2020. It transpired that overnight, many time zones away in California, the decision had been made to call off the BNP Paribas Masters at Indian Wells, one of the most significant events outside the Grand Slams. That was the preface for one of the most traumatic weeks in sporting history as, over the coming days, event after event was called off in the face of the coming Covid tsunami.

That Monday lunchtime I was travelling down to Cheltenham to help cover the classic horse-racing festival, which was to go ahead amid a sea of controversy. On the journey down a phone call came in from someone closely involved with the All England

Club: 'At Wimbledon it's already reckoned that it's only fifty–fifty that the tournament will happen this year,' they said. Given that Britain was only recording its third death from the virus that day, we agreed that this sounded somewhat alarmist and premature. Sure enough, on 1 April, The Championships of 2020 was cancelled, the blow being cushioned by an insurance policy.

Well before that, on 11 March, the World Health Organisation had declared a pandemic, and tennis players scattered around the globe were packing their bags and heading home. Every sport was to take a huge hit from Covid, but arguably none suffered more complications than tennis. It entered an extended period of hibernation, followed by a series of faintly dystopian events as it struggled to come back to normality. Its international dimensions, with players from multiple countries travelling to different territories week after week, made it something of a sitting duck for the virus. Nothing official would take place until the start of August and a WTA Tour event in the Sicilian capital of Palermo. It was here that the women's winner of Sunderland, Tomova, would become the first player to test positive at a tournament.

Raducanu, like everyone else, had no option but to hunker down at home and do her best with the online teaching provision from her school. She would try to keep fit by running around Bromley and, the following summer when she rose to prominence at Wimbledon, neighbours recalled that they had seen her doing some makeshift hitting in the cul-de-sac with her father. Matt James was on furlough and forbidden from doing any work with her, but he sent the occasional message to check that everything was okay.

As many tennis people pointed out at the time, there was hardly a sport around more suited to social distancing. One medic even suggested that the only danger from having a hit was if you physically stuck a ball in your mouth. Yet it was not until 13 May that clubs were allowed to open again for business. One stipulation was that players should use their own set of balls to serve with, and so avoid contaminating their opponent at the other end. Later in the week the National Tennis Centre was opened for elite training, again under strict guidelines.

By June a few unofficial tournament series, such as Novak Djokovic's ill-fated Adria Tour in the Balkans (abandoned after becoming a super-spreading event), were getting under way. The Lawn Tennis Association, meanwhile, was working on providing some domestic competitive opportunities for Britain's elite players while international travel restrictions remained in place. Some of that was done in conjunction with the entrepreneurial Jamie Murray, who had come up with the idea of staging 'Battle of the Brits' events supported by sponsors.

Less high-profile were tournaments organised purely under the LTA banner in the form of the British Tour. Although Raducanu was now in the midst of what would be a fifteen-month hiatus from playing world-ranking tennis, she did manage to play competitively in that period, at seven different events in all. Most went completely unnoticed by anyone other than the game's most ardent followers (or gamblers), hence the understandable perception among more casual fans that she almost totally vanished in this time.

Her first appearance back on court came in early July 2020, in the week which should have seen the start of Wimbledon. While Sue Barker and company were staging a daily BBC show from a studio at SW19 looking back on great memories from The Championships, a British Tour event was going on at **Roehampton**. Under strict supervision, some of the country's better prospects gathered and Raducanu was to reel off four victories and emerge the winner. A first match, interrupted by squally rain, was won against Emily Appleton 4–6, 6–3, 10–8.

Philippe Dehaes, the Belgian coach who had been advising her, was effectively stranded at home and, realistically, unable to travel over to London for the foreseeable future. As a result, former Davis Cup player turned TV commentator and coach Mark Petchey had been brought in to do some extra on-court work with Raducanu. As tennis was largely off the screens he was available, while making clear that he would have to return to his contractual duties when required. His main memory from being present for that encounter against Appleton was not so much the match as what she came armed with beforehand.

'Emma turned up with an A4 sheet of paper with all this stuff on it that was the most complicated thing I had ever seen. I couldn't understand a lot of it,' admits Petchey. 'It was her game plan in remarkable detail, complete with colour coding. To be honest, I never thought that anyone could take that much information with them out on court and execute it. What it told you, though, was that here was somebody diligent about her pre-match preparations, how much she had thought about it, and how seriously she was going to take this as a career.'

Fellow British youngsters Lissey Barnett and Amarni Banks were beaten in the next rounds and in the final she saw off Jodie Burrage in a sudden-death 'Champions' tiebreak 10–4, in blustery conditions, to win the week.

With such a light tournament schedule came the chance to make some changes which might benefit Raducanu in the long run. Petchey consulted with both Dehaes and Spaniard Esteban Carril (who had previously brought about so much improvement in Jo Konta's game). Their feeling was that her serve needed more work and that she might benefit from examining her racket options.

Trying out a Yonex as opposed to her usual Wilson, they found it added extra power but had the disadvantage of excessively flattening out the trajectory of the ball off her backhand. After more experimenting, the decision was made over July and August to make adjustments to her Wilson model, with a quarter of an inch added to the length and slightly more weight put on the frame. More emphasis was placed on closing the racket head at the point of impact on serve and raising the elbow higher when hitting the forehand.

'The thinking was that the slightly longer racket is definitely going to help your serve and it's going to help you out in the corners. I also thought she needed some more weight of shot,' recalls Petchey. 'It was an interesting time. It's not an easy fix, but Emma applied herself. It's not often you have the luxury of that, having time to change your game and your racket to become a better player, and do it without too many matches having to be played.'

He enjoyed working with Raducanu, who he describes as 'very mature for her age'.

'I think she's just curious about life. I am as well, and I really liked that aspect of her. She's very focused on court, but outside it she is interested in a lot of things, with wide-ranging views on loads of different stuff, and that appealed to me.'

He also enjoyed working with her father, whose views on coaching were reckoned to be unconventional by many in the game. His pick-and-mix approach to gleaning knowledge stretched to believing that certain coaches should be chosen to work for their expertise on certain shots.

'I'd say Ian is a very intelligent person who probably thinks a bit outside the box for some people that have spent the majority of their life in tennis, maybe doing things in a certain way they are used to. I felt like I was working with somebody who was very independent, and was keen to challenge you. He doesn't just accept everything a coach tells him.'

Petchey also gives a fascinating insight into the unorthodox approach of Ian Raducanu when it came to instilling professional habits in his daughter. One morning she arrived for practice, and upon opening her racket bag found a large bag of potatoes inside it.

'She was standing there pulling these potatoes out and we were just laughing about it. It was all about teaching her to pack her bag properly, which some young players can be sloppy about – that was the whole premise behind it and she understood. It was like, "You've got a bag that is four kilos heavier than it was yesterday, but you haven't even noticed it." I thought that was smart.'

By now Jamie Murray was planning to follow up his initial **Battle of the Brits** male-only offering with a mixed-sex team event running from 27 July until 2 August, again at Roehampton. It was natural that Emma would be one of the twenty-six all-British men and women invited to play in two scratch thirteen-a-side teams. One was the 'Union Jacks', captained by Judy Murray and Greg Rusedski, and the other the 'British Bulldogs', skippered by Leon Smith and Anne Keothavong. While there was no particular criterion for the line-ups, no spectators and no media allowed, the atmosphere between the two squads of competition-starved players became surprisingly feisty. Outsiders might have struggled to understand why emotions ran high at times, but players formed instant loyalties. British No. 1 Konta, selected for the Bulldogs, felt that some of the courtside sledging crossed the line on occasion.

Yet the large majority seemed to be enthused by it, and were to agree that the environment was beneficial in sharpening them up ahead of the looming US Open, after months of relative inactivity. For Raducanu this provided a rare chance to play doubles, as she teamed up for two mixed matches with GB men's No. 1 Joe Salisbury. Playing doubles was something that she had consciously avoided – another aspect which marked a different approach to her contemporaries. As at the end of 2021, she had still not played one doubles match at a professional event, and she only played seven doubles matches in total during her whole junior career at official ITF events. Many players use the format to help develop their volleying skills, but she had largely opted out.

Asked about this in October 2021 while at the Transylvania Open, she replied, 'I actually enjoy playing doubles, but the thing is when I am playing tournaments, because I haven't really played that many, I physically think I need to focus on singles. If I was to play both, I don't know how it would go. I just don't have much volume left in me for training, so after a few more years, a bit more work done, I'll probably start playing [doubles] a bit, because I enjoy it.'

Alongside Salisbury in the Battle of the Brits in 2020 she won one mixed-doubles match and lost the other. In her five singles matches she defeated Burrage, Katie Boulter and Naomi Broady, while also losing a match to Burrage, and Heather Watson as well. She ended up on the winning side as the Bulldogs – who featured Konta, Cam Norrie and Kyle Edmund among others – triumphed by 63 points to 56.

Jamie Murray, who combined organising the event with playing, was left with a very positive impression of someone he had not really encountered before: 'I had seen her practise at the NTC, but that's not the same thing as playing a match,' he said. 'But I think to go into an event like that where Andy [Murray] is competing and Jo [Konta], Heather [Watson], Dan [Evans] and Cam [Norrie], competing with them either in the singles or mixed doubles, the biggest thing was the way that she carried herself. She had a self-assurance, not in an arrogant way or anything, just very confident, and for some-body that young I thought that was really impressive. There was a lot of chat in that event, as well. It wasn't always easy to step on court and just compete, because you were getting it from all sides. But she was brilliant the whole week. I think she herself really enjoyed it. To be part of that I think helped a lot of them in terms of getting back out on tour and competing, and I think a lot had good results from being a part of that event.'

Her captain for the week, Keothavong, felt similarly: 'There was a lot of banter flying around, with each team trying to get under the other's skin, and it didn't bother Emma at all. Actually, I think she thrived on it. She was just happy to be out competing again.'

Unlike with some of the bigger names at the Battle of the Brits event, because her official ranking was still below 300 there was no US Open and its preparatory events for Raducanu to look forward to later that summer. Instead, her search for playing opportunities took her to the final week of the UK Pro League. Organised independently of the LTA, it was made up of a series of events that ran from early July to mid-August at St George's Hill in **Weybridge**. The format allowed the Kent teenager to come in for the finals week.

There she played world No. 147 Harriet Dart in the semifinals. There are virtually no recorded instances of Raducanu getting involved in heated battles that feature bad blood with an opponent, but her 6–0, 6–3 thrashing of the more experienced British player appears to have been one of those rare occurrences. An account of the match on the event's official website reported that 'Dart's patience was tested throughout the match as she struggled for the form that saw her reach the third round at Wimbledon last year, littering her game with unforced errors as Raducanu blew her away. Dart allegedly had regular pops at both her opponent and the umpire but Raducanu, still a teenager, says she thrives under that atmosphere.'

It quoted the winner as saying, 'It did get a bit intense and there were a few comments. In the heat of the battle you say and do things that you don't necessarily mean, so you can't really look that deep into it. A lot of the stuff was at her end so I couldn't hear, and I just heard from my coach that there were a lot of comments. She would walk past me and she would say something under her breath. I couldn't make out what she was saying, but when that happens they're under pressure. That's how I take it – when they're coming out with all of this stuff trying to disrupt your rhythm, I take it as they're trying to vent their energy and they're just channelling into me. So she was actually feeling the pressure, and I was enjoying it.'

For her part, Dart responded, 'I got stuffed love and three, so I'm not sure how it could be tense. I'm not going to dwell on this at all. It's one match and one match doesn't define you. Your ranking defines where you're at. It will be interesting once we get back to the main tour.' As luck had it, she would be Raducanu's opponent on her return to the official circuit, nearly ten months later at Nottingham.

Having beaten Dart, Raducanu played regular adversary Jodie Burrage in the final at St George's Hill, coming back from 2–6 in the first-to-10 deciding tiebreak to win it 10–8. That success also brought her best payday thus far, as she took home just over £15,000 in prize money.

Whatever progress Raducanu was making, it seemed to have passed Heather Watson by as the summer of 2020 came and went. The French Open had been controversially moved to a once-only late September/early October date, having been postponed from its usual springtime slot. It was not a happy event for the British contingent in cold, sluggish autumnal clay-court conditions. The usual inquest ensued as all six singles players from across the Channel lost in the first round. After her match Watson, one of the GBers ranked consistently high enough to gain entry to the Grand Slams, gave a bleak assessment of the elite British game.

'For me, as far as the next generation goes, Jo [Konta] is twenty-nine, I'm twenty-eight, Dan [Evans] is thirty, Norrie is younger. Apart from that, I don't really see who's next,' she said, after losing to French player Fiona Ferro. 'I don't see who's going to be top-fifty. I think personally that more players need to get help, rather than just helping your selected players. I don't know how many there are, but a handful of players. I feel like there needs to be a bigger pool of support.'

Asked about talented younger players coming through, and what could be done to nurture them, she responded, 'What younger players? I don't have anyone to talk about.'

In fairness to Watson, it was a post-match press conference held when emotions were running high, and in the wake of a disappointing defeat. It is nonetheless instructive in showing that no likely future star was considered to be waiting in the wings. While most people plugged in to the British game were aware of Raducanu's long-term potential, it has to be said there was no great chorus of 'What about Emma Raducanu?' in response to Watson's assertion.

By this time she had retreated into the shadows again, continuing with her A-level studies and having little inclination to travel to the smaller tournaments which were beginning to sprout up, albeit in the face of logistical struggles amid the ongoing pandemic. There was certainly no pressure coming from within her family. Instead, Nigel Sears did some sessions with her back in England during the Paris fortnight, while as autumn turned to winter there was more practice with Matt James, Petchey and former GB player Ed Corrie.

'I think her dad has a very measured approach to things,' reflects Sears. 'He is not one to rush in, and he is cautious. He knows she needs to protect her body. He didn't feel, quite wisely at times, that it was right to risk travelling unnecessarily during Covid. There weren't that many meaningful tournaments for her to play. The ITF calendar was challenging at best, and obviously there were issues with travel; she was still at school. So he's never over-pressed for her to play a huge number of tournaments.'

She re-emerged for a small flurry of activity just prior to Christmas 2020, when the National Tennis Centre at Roehampton was allowed to host more domestic events. These were held again under strict regulations, with Boris Johnson having just announced a new lockdown. First there was a much-reduced **British Tour 'Masters'** event that offered some competitive opportunities for UK players. Having received a walkover in the semi-final, she played a nominal final, against Amarni Banks, which was won 6–1, 6–4.

Immediately afterwards, running from 20 to 23 December, came a reprise of Murray's **Battle of the Brits** project, this time in the form of a mini-league separately for men and women. Raducanu achieved wins over Katy Dunne and Eden Silva before losing a tight match 3–6, 6–3, 10–2 against Heather Watson. Those present recall that one topic of conversation that week involved the question of whether too many voices were in her ear discussing the technicalities of her serve. She ended, unmemorably, third in the competition.

And so dawned 2021, the year in which Emma Raducanu's life would be turned on its head. Not that she or anyone else would have had any inkling of that, based on its first four months. Tennis once again returned to its place on the back burner as she spent the short winter days with her head buried in her books. With people's lives in the UK so restricted, she made almost no concessions to her future career, bar some training runs around Bromley. In the parallel universe of the outside tennis world, a delayed Australian Open started in February, only to be disrupted by successive Covid issues. Some players, Watson among them, were forced into a fortnight's hard quarantine after being identified as close contacts of cases. Planned crowds in the first week disappeared as a result of a renewed outbreak. Eleven months into the pandemic, it was all about trying to get events on, come hell, high water and viral infections.

It would be wrong to say that she was completely ignoring what was happening in Melbourne. At the LTA the top players are given what they term a 'case manager', and for Raducanu it was former British No. 1 Jeremy Bates, head coach of women's tennis at the governing body. While a case manager might sound more like something from the Social Services sector, their purpose in this instance is to take an overview role, checking on a player's progress. During the Australian Open Bates was impressed, although not surprised, to receive a call from Raducanu asking to go through videos of some matches she had been watching on TV. Unable to meet face-to-face, they did some analysis together via Zoom to discuss what she could learn from what she had seen in Melbourne.

So while Raducanu was keeping an eye on the tennis world, her on-court activity at that time was pretty much zero, as she was to reflect on at the end of the season: 'January, February, March, I didn't pick up a tennis racket really,' she said. 'I think March the 18th was my first session on court in 2021. And so January, February, March I was literally just sat at my desk staring at a wall for nine hours a day. So I feel with where I am now I just need to really take it all in and enjoy it, because looking back at how far I've come, it's pretty surreal. Where I was at the beginning of year, I would have never thought this was possible.'

Although all young people's A-levels were disrupted in that academic year, Raducanu's main focus remained the course work and exams which would determine her grades. As the days became longer and tennis reopened, she stepped up her training in conjunction with all that. For her tennis a significant move came later on in April. That was when Nigel Sears found that he had more time on his hands after parting ways with his main charge, Anett Kontaveit, following the WTA event in Stuttgart. 'Anett and I agreed before the tournament that it would be our last together, and then that roughly coincided with Emma finishing her exams,' he said. 'I offered to go full time with her through to the end of the grass season and then we'd reassess.'

With so little recent tennis behind her it was made known that, to be considered for wild cards into forthcoming grass-court events, she would need to start playing matches. They made the decision to re-enter the competitive fray on 20 May, to no fanfare whatsoever, at the three-day British Tour event at the Connaught Club in **Chingford**, Essex. Such tournaments are considered a bridge to the international Futures events, tending to attract domestic players from national academies, top-level county performers and those who have been involved in the US college system or are looking to head in that direction. And, as it turned out, the 2021 US Open champion.

Along with everyone else, Raducanu dutifully paid her £25 entry fee as she set out to gain some much-needed competitive exposure after an absence of five months. Her first opponent of the year was Maddie Brooks, a twenty-three-year-old from Norfolk who had played at Lipscomb University in Tennessee. She was dispatched 6–1, 6–1. After a walkover in the quarter-finals, Raducanu faced Katherine Barnes, another player from East Anglia, known as a fiery competitor but with barely any experience of the professional game. To look at the YouTube video of that match is simply to marvel that one of the participants, just 112 days later, would be lifting the trophy on Arthur Ashe Stadium in New York.

At the time Barnes, a year older than Raducanu, had played six tournaments over recent years at Futures level, three of them at the well-known testing ground of Antalya. A fairly staggering footnote is that the week before, in the British Tour event at Woking, Barnes had lost to a twelve-year-old. That was Hannah Klugman from Surrey, who was being identified as an outstanding prospect for her age. On the hard courts of the Connaught there were no line judges or ballkids, not even an umpire. The soon-to-be Queen of Flushing Meadows played the match in leggings, and Barnes can be seen manually inputting the points on an old-fashioned flip scoreboard by the net post.

In the first set Raducanu repeatedly double-faulted, miscued her groundstrokes and struggled with her opponent's unorthodox, slapped forehand. Matters improved in the second set but she was to lose the deciding 'Champions' tiebreak, going down 6–1, 1–6, 10–8. It would not be unfair to say the whole thing had the feel of a parks match. The Kent player was to depart with £75 in prize money for making the semis, around £1.8 million less than she would be paid less than four months later in New York.

With the grass-court season looming, some players might have retreated to the practice court to sharpen up. Instead Raducanu, the following week, chose to put herself back on the line against more players with nothing to lose, whom she would expect to beat. And so she made the journey out to the Suffolk port of **Felixstowe**, for the next British Tour event. In what was the season's first indication of the way she could rapidly improve, more normal service was resumed. On early-season grass courts that had plenty of eccentric bounces, four young British hopefuls were seen off without the loss of a set, in what was a more substantial tournament with a bigger field.

Over in Paris, Roland Garros was under way, meaning that the main tour-level grass-court season leading in to Wimbledon was shortly to start. A first title of 2021, Felixstowe rather than the French Open, was in the bag.

'We were told she was an up-and-coming player,' Bill Cunnew, chairman of Felixstowe Lawn Tennis Club, was later to tell the *Ipswich Star* newspaper as he reflected on Raducanu's humble beginnings in the summer of 2021. That turned out to be something of an understatement.

Trying to take in the magnitude of her achievement after defeating Markéta Vondroušová in the second round at Wimbledon in 2021.

5

BREAKTHROUGH

Armed with a world ranking of 366 and the Felixstowe British Tour title, Emma Raducanu walked into the Nottingham Tennis Centre to begin her official grass-court campaign of 2021. It was early June and still a time of daily lateral-flow tests, social distancing, one-way walking systems and a player bubble at the hotel, but the UK was enjoying a glorious burst of summer sunshine. **The Viking Open** for both men and women was to be the curtain-raiser of a reduced tournament schedule prior to Wimbledon. The high costs of staging an event amid all the necessary Covid security measures had led the Lawn Tennis Association to cut down the usual pre-SW19 programme. The traditional event at Surbiton, for example, was among the casualties. Despite the shrunken playing options meaning more players chasing fewer wild cards, a belief in Emma Raducanu's talent had led to her being offered one into the main draw in the land of Robin Hood.

The women's event, taking place on the outskirts of the East Midlands city, had $250,000 prize money. That accorded it the status of being on the main WTA Tour, while the concurrent one for the men was merely at the upper end of the Challenger tier. For the Kent teenager, no longer technically a schoolgirl, it represented a first ever appearance at this level. Rather than the field of innocent hopefuls from shortly before on the Suffolk coast, the draw was populated by seasoned pros, with Jo Konta the top seed. The crowd was restricted to 25 per cent of the regular capacity, but after what had gone before in 2021 it felt like an approximation of normality, all helped by glorious weather.

A smattering of the British media, having been stymied by the restrictions still in place at the French Open, travelled for an opening day with a spring in the step for the start of the three-week approach into Wimbledon. Aside from anything else, the success or otherwise of how Nottingham was staged might be a pointer towards how many spectators would be allowed into the All England Club. This was the subject of much speculation at the time, with the UK government having the final say. Raducanu was on the opening-day card, scheduled for late in the afternoon and facing a rematch against Harriet Dart, ranked much higher at 143.

As it turned out, this would be one of the last matches Raducanu played in relative obscurity. A measure of her then marginal status was that the few scribes in attendance were paying more attention to matters elsewhere. In particular, it was the first high-profile appearance of Francesca Jones, the articulate twenty-year-old from Yorkshire, since she had made national headlines earlier in the year by qualifying for the Australian Open. Jones had a rare back story in that she was forging a career in spite of being born with ectrodactyly ecto-dermal dysplasia, a condition which sees her having three fingers on each hand and a total of seven toes.

Not just that, but there was Konta, by far Britain's most consistent female performer in recent years, talking about her return to action the following day. Also playing in the opening session was Katie Boulter, almost a local, who had been suffer-ing from long-term injury. Boulter was to beat her Spanish opponent, while Jones was edged out in three tight sets by another Iberian, Georgina García Pérez, in somewhat dramatic fashion. The British player left the court in a wheelchair after going into a full body cramp in the deciding set, tension and fatigue having caught up after her opponent took a controver-sial nine-minute injury timeout.

By the time Raducanu and Dart took to the main court there had already been plenty to write about. And their first-round match was to slide even further down the agenda when the result went the way that the rankings suggested. A highly focused Dart gained revenge for the defeat at Weybridge the previous summer. A 6–3, 6–4 victory took a regulation seventy-seven minutes, with the anxious-looking Raducanu winning less than 45 per cent of her service points.

This was not the form of someone poised to make such an impression at Wimbledon that she would be sharing pages, front and back, with England's footballers as they progressed through the Euros. Several weeks later at SW19, when she had shown her true capabilities, coach Nigel Sears was able to look back on that Nottingham match with disarming frankness. 'I'm not saying that nerves have never been an issue, because she actually froze against Harriet Dart on the centre court at Nottingham with about five people watching,' he recalled. 'That was the first match for a long time on anything like a big court. The Court Two experience at junior Wimbledon against Iga Świątek [in 2018] was the other occasion prior to that. She found herself on the centre court of Nottingham and nerves hit her; there was no doubt about it.'

The result posed a dilemma for Wimbledon's wild-card committee. This is the small group charged with the ever-vexatious task of deciding which players are deserving of a privileged free pass into the grass-court Grand Slam, in cases when their ranking is below the standard entry level. Not a year goes by when this does not throw up some controversy – it has been that way since they were first introduced in 1977. According to research by the *Financial Times* in 2021, nearly 650 singles wild cards had been given out by Wimbledon since then, three-quarters of them going to British players. Of those, only eighteen had seen the recipients progress beyond the second round. For those arguing that wild cards can be counter-productive, the most commonly cited example was that of Alex Bogdanovic, the once-promising British man who received eight of them around the early 2000s and always lost in the first round.

Wimbledon is different to the other three Grand Slams in that it is hosted at an independent private club, separate from the sport's governing body, the Lawn Tennis Association. While the All England Club and its tournament is by far the largest funder of tennis in Britain, it sits apart from the rest of the British game, unlike the Australian, French and US Opens. This lack of cohesiveness is widely seen as a contributing factor to the sport continually falling short of its potential in the UK. When it comes to wild cards, the LTA's coaching staff are only able to make recommendations to the All England Club, who have these valuable commodities in their gift. In 2021 a wild card offered not just the chance of earning hefty ranking points, but a minimum £48,000 first-round loser's money.

When it came to Raducanu's case the committee, which included Tim Henman and Anne Keothavong, were concerned about her lack of form and matches. Could she really be competitive and justify the golden ticket? When the initial batch of wild cards was announced after the Viking Open (eventually won by Konta), Raducanu was given a free pass into qualifying, but was not one of the handful of Brits allocated to the main draw, as twice men's champion Andy Murray was. Sears was among those unhappy at the decision involving his player, pointing to the likelihood that her improvement would be sharp in the next two weeks. (It also meant that she would miss out on playing the week before in Eastbourne, as it looked like she would be otherwise engaged at Wimbledon qualifying.)

With the LTA having the discretion to give wild cards into regular Tour events, she was still able to stay on in **Nottingham** and play the week after. That was because an additional $100,000 tournament was being put on there to give players more match time on the grass ahead of Wimbledon. The TV cameras and media had disappeared down to Queen's in London, but in their absence Raducanu gave a truer picture of what she could do, and how her level could lift itself from week to week. In the first round she played Australia's Storm Sanders, ranked 148 in the world, and beat her 7–6, 6–2. In the second round she faced Hungary's Tímea Babos, a former world No. 25 and Grand Slam doubles champion. Babos was duly defeated 6–3, 6–3.

By the time Raducanu played in the quarter-final – against Bulgaria's Tsvetana Pironkova – the committee at SW19 had relented, and when the next batch of wild cards came out she was bumped up from the qualifying event straight into the main draw. Pironkova, an expert grass-courter who had previously made Wimbledon's semi-finals, was to win a tight encounter 7–5, 7–6, but through her efforts that week the British player was now guaranteed a taste of the big time.

This was to be a Wimbledon unlike any other. Among the changes prompted by the pandemic was where players could stay, with the government requiring all of them to be billeted in the Park Plaza hotel by Westminster Bridge. That is only eight miles from the Raducanu family home, but once she began practising at the All England Club she was obliged to check in to the official 'bubble' accommodation.

In the build-up to the tournament the deep-rooted connections of Sears in the women's game were to prove particularly useful, as he was able to arrange hitting sessions with high-calibre players. Twice she was linked up to play with 2017 women's champion Garbiñe Muguruza, for example. When off court she would study how the big names went about their business. As she got increasingly used to the weight and consistency of the ball delivered from quality sparring partners, it was no surprise that her level began to move sharply upwards.

Yet Raducanu was just another face among the 256 singles players about to embark on the third Grand Slam tournament of the year. This would be the final time she would enter one of the Majors without anyone taking much notice beforehand. As the nation's attention was largely diverted to England's progress at the European Championships, the return of Wimbledon after two years was receiving less scrutiny than would have been the case in a non-football year. Far from having to fend off a barrage of pre-tournament interview requests, the only significant mention of Raducanu prior to the start of the fortnight came on the immediately preceding Sunday, in the *Sunday Times*, with Alyson Rudd doing a jaunty feature on her sitting down alongside her near contemporary, Jack Draper. Each was asked to describe the other, and he proved prescient when remarking that she was 'a great player, explosive, a good mover. She hasn't played a lot but when she does, she's going to get right to the top of the game.'

Konta had garnered far more column inches, but that Sunday night – the eve of The Championships – it was announced that she was withdrawing after catching Covid. It was unknown then, but she had played her last Wimbledon. Day one saw Draper the focus of attention as he took to the Centre Court to play world No. 1 and defending champion Novak Djokovic. On the slick new grass court he acquitted himself admirably, taking the first set before succumbing to the great Serb while showing signs of enormous promise.

Raducanu was due to make her entrance on the second day, playing on Court 17, but the match was postponed when rain set in. It was not until Wednesday teatime that she finally got on, switched to Court 18 as the schedule played catch-up. This is the quirky arena tucked between the broadcast facilities and Henman Hill, with limited seating down two sides and a banked area of seats at the end backing on to the hill. Most famous for hosting the historic marathon between Nicolas Mahut and John Isner in 2010, it was to be the scene of Emma Raducanu's full debut at the **Wimbledon Championships**.

Her opponent was Vitalia Diatchenko, a thirty-year-old ranked 150 in the world. It looked one of the kinder draws, although the Russian had won three matches to come through the qualifying event, and in 2018 had beaten two Grand Slam champions at the All England Club, Maria Sharapova and Sofia Kenin. Still ranked 188 places below her, Raducanu was very much second favourite, and the first game would not go against that argument.

Serving woes affected the nervous British debutante, who sent down four double faults in the opener, to get broken immediately. Thereafter it became far more competitive, although she had to save break points to avoid going 5–1 down. Coming back to force a tiebreak, and giving another early sign of how she could steady her nerve, she wrapped up an eighty-three-minute first set by taking it 7–4. That broke the Russian's spirit and the following set was won 6–0.

'It was just a nervy experience in the beginning, playing your first main-draw Grand Slam match at Wimbledon,' she admitted later. 'A lot of people there, you didn't want to let them down. I'm just really happy that I managed to find a way through the tough moments, then I settled in and started playing more relaxed. Everything is just a bonus to me right now.'

Still, with Katie Boulter coming close to beating second seed Aryna Sabalenka on the Centre Court – and with Andy Murray providing classic melodrama into the evening with a five-set win over qualifier Oscar Otte – Raducanu's achievement ended up as little more than a footnote to day three.

She was back in action twenty-four hours later, this time at the other end of the All England Club estate on Court 12, with her opponent the world No. 42, Markéta Vondroušová. To followers of the British game the name of the young Czech brings back painful memories of Roland Garros in 2019. It was there that she defeated Jo Konta in the semi-final of the French Open, a golden opportunity escaping for the then British No. 1. Konta, in command, had missed a straightforward drive volley on set point that grey morning in the French capital. It was a *Sliding Doors* moment – had that gone in, it is entirely possible she would have gone on to win a Grand Slam title and become the first British woman since Virginia Wade to do so.

Now the twenty-two-year-old Czech stood between the third round and the eighteen-year-old who would soon claim that distinction. With crowd restrictions still in place, there were many empty spaces in the stands, although a couple of school friends from Newstead Wood added to the numbers. Vondroušová's touch and variety proved no match for Raducanu's driven groundstrokes, each one of them struck with confidence. Although she needed to come back from 3–1 down in the second set, it seemed by now almost incomprehensible that one of these players was ranked 338 in the world. It must have helped that the slightly unorthodox Czech left-hander had been one of her practice partners in the build-up week.

As the last British woman standing at Wimbledon, this was where the recent A-level student really started to attract attention. Post-match press conferences were being conducted in an empty interview room, via Zoom, but there were plenty of faces up on the large screen she was looking at. The winner was asked if she would trade A-star grades in her exams for a fourth-round place. 'I'd have to say round four of Wimbledon,' she replied. 'I think anyone that knows me would be like, "What?" Everyone thinks I'm absolutely fanatical about my school results. Actually, I would say I have high standards for myself. That's helped me get to where I am in terms of tennis and also in terms of school results. I'd still pick round four.'

The middle Saturday of Wimbledon arrived with former LTA talent scout Simon Dahdi preparing for a weekend shift driving his train into London. He was also thinking about his former job, as the young girl he had first spotted on a mini-tennis court was due to play in the third round of Wimbledon on Court One.

Her opponent was the seasoned Sorana Cîrstea of Romania, a thirty-one-year-old who had made her Wimbledon debut when Raducanu was just five. Twice in the previous three Grand Slams she had beaten Konta. Now, the veteran broke her much younger opponent to take a 3–1 lead, but then came the kind of roll with which we were to become familiar at Flushing Meadows. The teenager from Bromley Tennis Centre reeled off the next eight games.

'I was driving a train at the time on my route into London Blackfriars with Thameslink,' recalls Dahdi. 'Of course when you're driving into London, you need to have your phone switched off. When I got there I switched it on again and she was nearly a set up and I was like, "Wow, this is unbeliev-able." On the return journey I had to have my phone turned off again and it was so frustrating, I couldn't find out what was happening. After a couple of stops I thought, "I'm going to make an announcement here, I need to find out what's going on." So I put the Tannoy on and said, "If anyone's able to come to the front of the train when we stop at the next station, please update me with the score from the Emma Raducanu match at Wimbledon." At every stop, people would come down to the front and give me the score. Finally, a few stops further on, some guy told me that she had won. It was a great feeling.'

After match point was sealed, to the rousing acclaim of the arena, BBC commentator Nick Mullins gave his verdict: 'British tennis has a new star, Wimbledon has a new star, and we have just heard one of the sporting roars of the year.'

For making the last sixteen she was now guaranteed £181,000, dwarfing the £28,000 she had made from official prize money prior to that. The story and the smiles that accompanied it were now captivating the public: 'Yesterday I came out here and I sat courtside for about five minutes. I knew what to expect a little bit. And I thought if you're not going to enjoy Court One at Wimbledon, home crowd, what are you going to enjoy? This is the cherry at the top of tennis,' said Raducanu.

The fact that she was now the only British singles player going into the second week – Cam Norrie and Dan Evans had lost that day – only heightened the thirst for knowledge about someone who, a week previously, was barely known beyond hardcore fans.

Prior to the Cîrstea match, Nigel Sears had been asked about her potential, and he did not hold back: 'Whenever she has performed, her win–loss ratio is pretty good,' he said. 'She doesn't have much match experience, that's the impressive thing. To be able to win matches at Challengers is one thing. To step up and play seasoned pros on a big stage is quite another. She has an analytical mind, which she gets from her dad, and her mum has always been in her corner in terms of the academic side. I just think she's very ambitious, so when she thinks about professional tennis, she's not thinking about being an also-ran on the tour. She wants to do something. She doesn't consider professional tennis as just going out there and you play some tournaments on the tour for a few years.

She's all about achieving. That's what I mean by thinking big. She's not easily impressed. And she is a smart girl. So she's fully aware of who's out there, what's out there, because she watches a lot of tennis.

'I think Emma compares very, very favourably in terms of material. I always have felt that, from day one. She has the necessary qualities and she's hungry enough and eager to learn. Given the right opportunities and more match experience, I think she'll make good progress. It's really up to her how far she goes. Quite frankly, I think the sky's the limit.'

The bullish nature of his comments raised the odd eyebrow among reporters. A couple of us wondered out loud if that had been a rare instance of the press thinking a coach might be talking a player up excessively, rather than the other way round. Sears, however, was to be proved correct in his assessment, quicker than anyone thought.

Now facing an unexpected second weekend in the Park Plaza bubble, Raducanu jokingly pointed out that she would have to do some emergency laundry as she was running out of clean clothes.

She was to be the last British singles player who would ever be involved in a 'Manic Monday' at Wimbledon. Later in the summer, the All England Club announced that it was bringing in play for fourteen straight days, wiping out the fallow Sunday and avoiding the need for all fourth-round singles to be played the following day in a packed programme. That will go some way to ensuring that the controversy which was to ensue in 2021 will not be repeated.

Wimbledon has traditionally cast itself as an 'outdoor, daytime' event but, like many of the old ways down at SW19, that has become increasingly blurred by the mission creep of modern sporting commerce. With the ink starting to dry on a new TV contract with the BBC worth north of £60 million a year – not to mention arrangements with international broadcasters – the attraction of big matches being played before an evening audience, when people are home from work, was ever more alluring.

This had become an unspoken trend, and Andy Murray had already filled the prime-time slot twice in the first week. Now, the new darling of Wimbledon found herself scheduled as the last match on Court One, against Australian Ajla Tomljanović. The timing itself seemed to be a clear departure from the old patrician attitude towards setting the order of play with fairness to the players at its heart.

With the women's quarter-finals programmed for Tuesday, none of the eight fourth-round matches was slated to start after mid-afternoon at the latest – except for the one that people most wanted to see. The winner was due to face either Australian Ash Barty or Barbora Krejčíková of the Czech Republic, but they were due off at 1 p.m. Raducanu and Tomljanović would, uniquely, have to wait for the end of the men's match between Alex Zverev and Félix Auger-Aliassime before bringing up the rear of the women's schedule.

Fatefully, it turned out that the match between the German Zverev and his Canadian opponent would go the full distance,

'Who, me?' – Emma Raducanu can't contain her joy and surprise after beating home favourite Shelby Rogers in the fourth round of the 2021 US Open.

Above: Another product of the Bromley Effect, Naomi Cavaday – here in her playing days at Surbiton in 2007 – was an influential early coach.

Left: A young Emma Raducanu on her way to the semi-final of an international Under-12 tournament in Auray, France, in March 2014.

Below left: Making the short trip to SW19 in 2017 for her debut in the junior tournament, where she was thrilled to secure a selfie with Roger Federer.

Below: Renee Raducanu celebrates as the years of hard work and support are rewarded at Wimbledon in 2021.

Starting to rack up the air miles – to play in the 2019 junior Australian Open.

A rare chance to play doubles – teaming up with Joe Salisbury in the Battle of the Brits tournament at Roehampton in July 2020.

A low-key return to the official tour in June 2021 – a first-round loss at Nottingham to Britain's Harriet Dart, a regular opponent on the circuit.

A few weeks later, on her full debut at Wimbledon, early nerves are swiftly overcome in a straight-sets win over Vitalia Diatchenko.

The last British woman standing, Emma Raducanu performs on Wimbledon's Court One for the first time, facing Romania's Sorana Cîrstea in the third round.

The much more experienced Cîrstea had made her Wimbledon debut when Raducanu was just five. Now she was swept away by the kind of roll that would become familiar at the US Open.

'Wimbledon has a new star . . . and we have just heard one of the sporting roars of the year' – the crowd goes wild as the 18-year-old defeats Cîrstea to reach the last 16 in July 2021.

'The sky's the limit' – enjoying that winning feeling with coach Nigel Sears.

Breathing difficulties bring a premature end to her fourth-round match against Australia's Ajla Tomljanović – after a draining wait for the end of a marathon men's match on 'Manic Monday'.

'It appears it just got a little bit too much' – John McEnroe's comments on Raducanu's withdrawal were seen as unwelcome by many, while others preferred to criticise the controversial scheduling.

The trip of a lifetime begins – serving to Zhang Shuai of China in San Jose, California, in August 2021, the first leg of a vital spell on the US hard-court circuit, accompanied by her new coach, Andrew Richardson (*below*).

taking a marathon four hours and two minutes to complete. While the victorious Barty had walked off court to prepare for her quarter-final at 2.42 p.m., Raducanu and Tomljanović ended up walking on at 7.53 p.m.

Tennis differs from the large majority of high-profile sports in that, apart from those slated first on the daily schedule, its open-ended nature means that matches begin at an indeterminate time. For most contests there is no pre-ordained kick-off to build up to or, as in golf, a precise tee time to prepare for. Handling this takes experience, and the more travelled players become familiar with what suits them best to cope. It involves adjusting an individual's eating time, stretching and warm-ups. Over time someone like Murray, for instance, has seen it all and learned what works best for him.

Raducanu had never been in that position for an occasion as big as this – she was even unfamiliar with playing at night under lights. As the tension rose throughout the day, ahead of a match many were predicting her to win, she stationed herself around the Aorangi Park practice complex. As a lowly wild card, this was where her locker room was, away from the elite dressing rooms housing the seeds in the Centre Court. She did her best to sequence her eating and practice, but with Zverev and Auger-Aliassime pushing each other deeper into five sets this was, in all senses, completely new territory.

Eventually her match was called, and the two players walked out in front of an expectant crowd now at 75 per cent capacity, as government regulations for the main show courts had been relaxed. Sitting anonymously in the crowd were Ian and Renee

Raducanu, who had been unable to see their daughter close up in person all tournament, because mixing with anyone outside the player bubble was outlawed. Supporting Tomljanović vigorously from the player box was her boyfriend, Matteo Berrettini, who would go on to reach the men's final.

Through a tight first set there was little to choose between the players, but at 4–4 the twenty-eight-year-old Australian managed to stave off two break points. She then broke to take the first set 6–4, and it soon became clear that her young opponent was struggling at the start of the second. Raducanu's distress became increasingly obvious as she reached for the towel between points.

The tour physio was summoned on by umpire Aurélie Tourte and a stethoscope was applied to Raducanu's back as she sat in the courtside chair, her chest heaving. Away from the white heat of Wimbledon's glare, such incidents, while not commonplace, have been seen plenty of times before around the circuit. Jo Konta and former world No. 1 Victoria Azarenka had been among those temporarily overwhelmed on court during matches elsewhere in preceding years. Nonetheless, there was shock among the crowd witnessing the unfolding scene.

At 0–3 Raducanu was escorted off and a few minutes later, to gasps from the assembly, assistant referee Denise Parnell emerged to instruct the umpire, who in turn announced that the British player would not be returning. Word came through later that Raducanu was recovering, and a bald statement was issued that the retirement was due to 'breathing difficulties'.

The British singles challenge at Wimbledon, coming from such an unlikely source, was over for another year. Its breakout star had not even made it to the Centre Court. As for Tomljanović, she had to be back in action less than twenty-four hours later, and could manage only four games against the contrastingly rested Barty.

In the first match of her American tour, at San Jose in California in early August 2021, Emma Raducanu shows the determination that would bring her unexpected success the following month.

6

THE TRIP OF A LIFETIME

The morning after the night before at Wimbledon began with Anne Keothavong, captain of Britain's Billie Jean King Cup team, updating listeners of BBC Radio 4 that the stricken player was feeling much better. Meanwhile the social media platform of Twitter (bringing out the best in everyone as ever) was still convulsed by the events of the previous evening.

The comments of TV's star analyst John McEnroe were the subject of particular attention. Having watched matters unfold on Court One, he had said, 'I feel bad for Emma. It appears it just got a little bit too much, as is understandable . . . I don't think it helped that the previous match went as long as it did because it made her think about it more. That's a lot to take on, especially when you've never been there before.'

Some took offence on Raducanu's behalf, and soon the likes of Piers Morgan and Gary Lineker were weighing in from different angles. This temporary upstaging of the England football team in the national discourse was proof that the recent A-level student was now very big news indeed. A further indication came via one very modern measure: having gone into The Championships with 2,000 Instagram followers, she was now up to 255,000.

Also causing continued discussion was the scheduling – exacerbated by the length of the Zverev–Auger-Aliassime match. Paul McNamee, former Wimbledon doubles champion and once the man in charge of both the Australian tennis and golf Opens, had summed up in a tweet what some others were thinking. In response to a Wimbledon statement that all decisions are made 'with fairness and the best interests of the tournament, players, spectators and our worldwide broadcast audience at heart', he expressed his disagreement: 'Doesn't do it for me . . . all women's singles matches had to be first, and worst case second, as it's the only day they are scheduled to back up [Monday to Tuesday] . . . a simple "sorry" would have sufficed.'

It had been the most difficult Championships on record to organise, and Wimbledon had done an excellent job overall, but this episode was probably not the fortnight's finest hour.

The last word needed to be with Raducanu herself who, after taking a precautionary PCR test, cheerfully resurfaced that afternoon. In the atrium of the Park Plaza an interview studio had been set up, and she appeared wearing an England football shirt. Speaking to the BBC's Sue Barker, she did not really contradict what McEnroe had suggested, in a frank and good-humoured reflection: 'I found it very difficult to regulate my breathing. It was emphasised by some long rallies we had towards the end of the first set which made it tough for me to keep my composure and breathing in check. At the beginning of the second set was when I was struggling with it the most, and I called the trainer on. I don't know what caused it. I think it was a combination of everything that has gone on behind the scenes and the accumulation of the excitement and the buzz.' It had been, she added, the best week of her life and a great learning experience. The following evening she was at Wembley, watching England beat Denmark to make the final of the Euros.

Raducanu had one more commitment to fulfil, and that was her promise to take the team who had helped her that fortnight out for a steak dinner in central London. Booking the restaurant herself, she entertained physio Tom Cornish, physical trainer Gareth Shelbourne, coach Nigel Sears and Chris Helliar, who had been brought into her management team by IMG.

Thoughts were quickly turning towards what was to come, and the different possibilities that were opening up. Having entered the grass-court season with a ranking of 366, the vague plan had been to play some smaller events on the ITF circuit in southern Europe once the grass was done, furthering the gradual development process. Now up to 179, a place in the US Open qualifying event was already guaranteed for late August, so it would make more sense to orientate herself towards that.

She was not quite finished at Wimbledon, turning up on the Sunday to watch the men's final alongside Jane O'Donoghue, one of the coaches who had been instrumental in her growth. Together they watched Novak Djokovic take the title.

The few days and weeks after her exit allowed for a mix of business and pleasure. The following weekend gave her the chance to indulge her passion for motor sport. In accordance with her new status, she was given a VIP invitation to the British Grand Prix at Silverstone, joining fellow VIP guests such as Tom Cruise (who had become a curiously permanent fixture at the British summer of sport) and Prince Edward. As part of the experience Raducanu was given a lap of the circuit in a McLaren supercar, thrilling in the passenger seat as a professional driver took her round the circuit at speeds of up to 160 miles per hour. More sedately, a couple of days later she paid a return visit to her alma mater of Bickley Primary School to meet some of the pupils there.

On the business front, decisions had to be made about the programme of tournaments going forward, and who would be accompanying her on a schedule now pivoting towards the hard courts of America. The arrangement with Sears expired on the last day of Wimbledon and he was informed that, despite the fourth-round showing, his player would be looking elsewhere for coaching. With the attention of the sporting world moving on very quickly from SW19 to such things as the Formula One and the Olympics, it was not until the US Open that she had the platform to explain a move that took some observers aback.

'I really respect Nigel and we got on great, but at this stage of my career a fresh voice and ear is good,' she said. 'He [Sears] is very good at the top end, and that's where he probably brings the most value.'

By the estimation of her and her father, after Wimbledon she was not yet at the level where Sears was most used to working. Indeed, her ranking was still far off gaining her direct entry into the Grand Slams. There was also the consideration that she was about to embark on what was to be her longest trip away from home, as the American itinerary was taking shape. A key component of this was that IMG could use its clout to facilitate the award of a wild card into one of the first events of the US summer, the Mubadala Silicon Valley Classic, in the northern California city of San Jose, starting on 2 August. The reason was simple: they owned it. From the tournament's point of view, Raducanu's entry would add some lustre to the field; from their client's standpoint, it offered the chance of more top-level experience.

Ever prepared to venture beyond the parameters of conventional thinking when it came to coaches, the Raducanus had settled on a surprise candidate to accompany her – Andrew Richardson.

The connection dated back to Raducanu's early development when she began training in earnest at the Bromley Tennis Centre. He was one of several coaches who had helped hone her game, and their deep-rooted association was appealing for a trip of this nature. Given that they would be spending weeks upon end together, a strong personal chemistry would be essential. Aside from recognising his phlegmatic nature, she also rated his technical know-how. Above all, it showed the value the family placed on a specific fit for the prevailing set of circumstances.

What he was not, and would not have claimed to be, was someone with a hugely current knowledge of the women's circuit at the top level and just below. Richardson had been a professional player through the 1990s, a direct contemporary of Tim Henman. While not possessing his friend's exceptional ability, he was definitely among the more gifted of that age group. His signature was a potent serve delivered from his left hand from the great height afforded by his 6 ft 7 in stature. Known as 'Flex' due to his body shape and telescopic limbs, he had always been a notably popular figure around the British scene. While he was no pushover, and had firm ideas about the game, there was also an element of the gentle giant.

It could be argued that his temperament was not ideally suited to the harsh environment of playing a one-on-one sport and, unlike Henman, he was not able to fulfil his early potential. He had peaked just inside the world's top 100 in doubles, but never got beyond 133 in singles. The year of 1997 was when he best showed his possibilities, reaching the third round at Wimbledon, where he lost to Greg Rusedski. Earlier that season he had played his best ever match, defeating the then world No. 46, the nuggety Byron Black of Zimbabwe, over five gutsy sets in a Davis Cup match at Crystal Palace. Hopes that this would prove a launch pad towards greater things eventually dissipated.

As in a lot of sports, the downside of being an empathetic character during a playing career can be a contrasting advantage when it comes to the emotional intelligence that coaching demands. After his days as a pro had come to an end in 2000 he had worked mainly domestically as opposed to internationally, and his coaching at the elite end had often been with British men. Since his time spent with Raducanu at Bromley he had largely been the head coach of the elite tennis programme at Culford School in Suffolk. Over seven years Richardson had helped establish it as one of the leading schools for tennis in the country. It had become one of the LTA's Regional Player Development Centres.

Earlier in 2021 he had chosen to move on and relocate with his family to south-west London. One factor was the freedom to take one of his young sons, showing promise as a player, away on trips to events without having to prioritise his wider responsibilities to the programme at Culford. He had maintained sporadic contact with Raducanu, but was not expecting the approach to take her through what was left of the summer. As it happened, fatefully, the dates for this winding trip around America, from late July until the end of August, were compatible with his domestic and family commitments. After some persuasion and discussion, and excited by the challenge, he agreed to take on the task of travelling with her around the United States.

One major upside was that there would now be a month in which, in contrast to her recent experience at Wimbledon, it would be possible to work in relative obscurity. The four planned stops before landing in New York – San Francisco, San Jose, Landisville and Chicago – involved three tournaments of the kind which might draw the odd local media representative, but nothing beyond that.

Before leaving, both parties were clear that the trip's purpose was far more about seeing an improvement in her game and physical level than racking up ranking points. If some wins came, then all well and good, but developing her for the longer term was the priority. As he was to recall on the night she lifted the trophy at Flushing Meadows: 'I said at the beginning, I am not going to judge this on results, more on performances and how much you put into every day. She really bought into that, so that's what we focussed on. I didn't have any goals as far as the results would go on the trip.'

A week was spent back at their old sparring venue of Bromley, hitting together on court to get ready. On 24 July 2021 this unlikely duo, just the two of them, flew out to California, embarking on the journey that would change their lives.

First stop for a training week was San Francisco, and more precisely the Hellman Tennis Complex, just across the bay north of Oakland. This is the home of the tennis team representing the University of California, Berkeley. As is fairly typical of the US college system, the facilities are high class. That is one reason why many of Raducanu's contemporaries in the British juniors ended up taking scholarships offered by American universities, seeing it as a possible bridge to a pro career while offering a decent education. At Berkeley they met up with Raymond Sarmiento, a twenty-nine-year-old Californian who had played to top-300 level on the ATP Tour, and who would act as a hitting partner for a few days.

Off court, Richardson began to discover that his charge's horizons were somewhat broader than you might expect in a teenage tennis player. Unlike many, she really did want to explore the city she found herself in, and her interest in archi-tecture was genuine. She posted a picture on Instagram of herself with the Golden Gate Bridge in the background, saying, 'Strauss' 1930s genius . . . pretty fascinating seeing for real after studying it in y8 d&t [Design and Technology].' Not only that but she also went to look at the city's Painted Ladies. These are the many houses in the area from the Victorian/Edwardian era famously adorned in bright colours.

The main business in hand, however, was tennis and after some hard sessions on court with Sarmiento it was time to make the hour's journey south to **San Jose**, where her wild card awaited. She drew the thirty-two-year-old world No. 51, Zhang Shuai of China, and the result was much less spectacular than anything seen at SW19. The form book was respected this time and the more experienced player ran out a 6–3, 6–2 winner.

'I am at the very beginning. It is my second [main] WTA Tour tournament. I am just learning and it is onwards from here,' she said. 'What I learned is how to try and deal with someone when they are playing very well and you feel like you are not doing much wrong but you are constantly on the back foot. That is not something I am used to at the levels I have played before. Stepping up to this, I feel she just dictated me. I didn't play badly, so I am just continuing with the hard work I am doing. If I keep going this way, at some point it will pay off.'

Now came the most gruelling part of the voyage, starting with the 3,000-mile journey by air across the United States to

Landisville in Pennsylvania. Not a great deal happens in this town of nearly 2,000 inhabitants, probably best known for being close to one of America's largest Amish populations. Yet it does hold an annual tennis event of reasonable size, sitting below the main WTA Tour and offering $100,000 in prize money. Five years previously a player with whom she was sometimes compared, Laura Robson, had won the title there.

A world ranking of 184 was enough for Raducanu to gain entry into the qualifying of an event sponsored by the local jewellers and very much part of the town's calendar. From the outset it was clear what the main challenge of the week would be – the heat. August is always steamy in those parts, but in 2021 there was a heatwave making the conditions brutal for all concerned. Every night there was a thunderstorm, and each following day it would build up towards a repeat. For a player who had yet to bank years of hard training it would be especially difficult.

Raducanu was not alone in finding it hard to adjust. She lost the first three games of her opening match in the preliminaries, against Korea's Na-Lae Han, but then reeled off the next twelve. Getting more used to the environment, she made it into the main draw with a straight-sets win over one-time world No. 21 Mona Barthel of Germany, who had slid to 213 at the time. If she was suffering in the combination of temperatures in the mid-thirties and acute humidity, then so were others. In the first round proper three players retired with heat exhaustion, with ten-minute breaks being introduced if matches were split at one set all.

The tough conditions were responsible for an incident which attracted considerable attention to a tournament which would normally go by almost totally unnoticed by the outside world. Former world No. 9 and twice Grand Slam semi-finalist CoCo Vandeweghe was playing Georgia's Ekaterine Gorgodze, and had won the first set. During the second she experienced breathing difficulties, appearing to concede its latter stages without making much effort. After the heat break at one set all, Vandeweghe came back out and appeared to decline to give her opponent a proper warm-up, lamely batting the ball back and sometimes switching the racket to her left hand. Video footage of the strange scene went viral and drew much criticism of her behaviour – it was an unwanted way for the Landisville event to plant itself on the map. Heavy rain then caused play to be abandoned for the day and Vandeweghe withdrew the following morning. She later explained her physical discomfort, and it turned out that she was within her rights when it came to the warm-up.

Meanwhile Raducanu had battled past Belgium's Ysaline Bonaventure in the first round and earned herself a meeting with Gorgodze for the next match. It was an important day for the Kent teenager in more ways than one, because that morning she was receiving her A-level results. Amid the Covid disruption Newstead Wood were basing these on actual exams taken, rather than purely on the assessment of course work, as was the case in some schools. She later explained in a feature with the WTA Tour's website that she had found learning mathematics remotely particularly challenging: 'It's tough to do on a computer when you can't show the teacher the problem in front of you,' she said.

Ever disciplined, she refused to look at the email containing her grades until she had played her second-round match against the twenty-nine-year-old Georgian. The scene could hardly have been more different from Wimbledon's Court One: on an outside court at bucolic Landisville with Richardson standing up courtside and leaning his rangy frame over the fence. Despite the searing humidity causing problems for both players, who were sometimes doubled up in pain and had to retreat to the shadows when possible, Raducanu fought back to ultimately demolish her opponent 3–6, 6–0, 6–1. It was a creditable result, but better was to come. After coming off court she allowed herself to look at the outcome of her A-levels – an A-star in Maths and an A in Economics. Those long days spent studying during lockdown over the first three months of the year, and long before that, had paid off.

Tennis-wise, however, the conditions that week were beginning to exact a heavy toll. The quarter-final was against Spain's Nuria Párrizas Díaz, and the weather had not relented. At 4–3 down, having evenly contested the first seven games, Raducanu walked to her chair and retired for the second time in three tournaments.

From the quaint charm of Landisville, the Raducanu–Richardson duo now headed west for the fourth week of their mini-odyssey to somewhere very different. The XS Tennis Village is on the south side of **Chicago**, not exactly an area you would associate with the sport born from garden parties and originally known as lawn tennis. Boasting the longest straight line of courts anywhere – twelve of them in a row – it is a place whose primary aim is to use the game as a way of improving the lives of disadvantaged young people.

In the third week of August it was hosting a tournament offering $125,000 in prize money, just below main-tour status, and the British player had been given a wild card into the main draw. A few more familiar faces were around, with the 2021 US Open coming up, Nigel Sears being one of them. This event was to be massively instrumental in toughening up the recent A-level student. It was clear that her tennis was improving by the week, but her body was struggling to keep up with the technical advancements. She arrived feeling weary and, although the temperatures were slightly less brutal than in Pennsylvania, it was still hot and there were several junctures when she came close to pulling out again. The temptation was to try and stay fresh for the following week and the main goal of qualifying for Flushing Meadows. That she chose the more difficult option of battling through matches was to prove enormously telling.

Not that a prolonged stay looked in the offing initially. Her first opponent was the top seed and world No. 58, Alison Van Uytvanck, who back in 2018 had looked on admiringly at her game on the Wirral. In a sign of what was to come, Raducanu outserved the highest-ranked player in the field, landing in two out of three of her first deliveries. In the next round she took out Clara Burel, the former world junior No. 1 who had beaten her on her one previous appearance in New York, in the juniors. Now her first-serve percentage was shading over 70, and she was wreaking havoc with her returns as well, winning seven out of ten points against second serve in that match. Her next opponent, German Jule Niemeier, retired after losing a first-set tiebreak.

Playing a third consecutive day, it took everything Raducanu had to beat American Claire Liu in two hours and forty-six minutes, 7–6, 4–6, 6–1. Having battled exhaustion, her biggest final to date had been reached, with her adversary now an old foe, Clara Tauson of Denmark. Given that the qualifying in Landisville had only started the previous Monday, it would mean a tenth match inside fourteen days. While she may not have appreciated it at the time, a few weeks later Raducanu was able to look back at that tightly packed catalogue of encounters and appreciate how invaluable it had proved.

'It helped a lot,' she said. 'I played some hard-court tournaments and they were very good for me to adjust, because it's completely different to the grass. I think that gradually building up the levels at the tournaments, my game got better. With each tournament I played, I had to raise my game. The amount of matches I had really helped with my confidence. I personally think that inside I knew I had some sort of level that was similar to these girls, but I didn't know if I was able to maintain it over a set or over two sets.'

In Chicago, her first final since Pune in December 2019 was to end in crushing disappointment, albeit against a highly rated contemporary who had accrued considerably more experience. With Raducanu struggling to control her serve in the wind, the first set was lost quickly. After coming back to win the second, she led 3–2 in the decider before the Dane took four of the last five games in front of the 250 spectators gathered. The battle between two teenagers was settled when Raducanu was broken at the end, to go down 6–1, 2–6, 6–4 in two hours and fifteen minutes.

It was enough, however, to move the British player up to 150 in the rankings, making her one of only four players born in 2002 to move inside that mark at the time. The question now was whether all that energy expended would hurt her in the New York qualifying. The answer was that nobody was to take a set off her again until October.

That night a mini-hurricane struck New York, backing up flights for the following day, but by lunchtime they were able to get out of Chicago. Before that, in the morning, Raducanu kept the long-time promise to herself that she would not leave the Windy City without visiting the metal Anish Kapoor sculpture in Millennium Park known as 'The Bean'. She duly did so, the requisite picture was taken to mark the occasion, and then it was off to the airport. New York was about to experience a different type of whirlwind.

Celebrating her dominant third-round win over Spain's Sara Sorribes Tormo at Flushing Meadows – the performance that really made the tennis world sit up and take notice.

7

NEW YORK

Englishmen in New York were thin on the ground during the 2021 **US Open**. Covid-induced travel restrictions meant that the city, usually a melting pot of nations, felt almost strangely parochial. Entering the United States was difficult for non-citizens without a valid work reason, and for some of us that meant both the possession of a pre-existing visa and a special exemption granted by the US embassy.

Nowhere did Manhattan seem more hollowed out than Midtown. Along Fifth Avenue the crowds were gone from Trump Tower and at Central Park the horses and traps ferrying tourists around had largely disappeared. The vast rectangle was peopled only by locals and a few visitors from out of state. The traffic and pavements often had the sense of this being a holiday weekend of normal times. Down on Lexington Avenue, hotel after hotel was still closed because of the pandemic. Across the road from where the fleet of tournament buses would ferry players and staff out to Queens there was a daily reminder of the situation: the huge central Marriott was simply boarded up. At many of the eating and drinking establishments that were familiar haunts to us journalists – Bill's, Hudson's, the Pig and Whistle – you could do no more than peer through the dusty windows and see the chairs stacked up on top of each other in the dark. In those that were still open, proof of vaccination was increasingly being sought.

Among the places where it was, reassuringly, business as usual was the twenty-four-hour Smiler's Deli on the corner of 54th Street and Madison Avenue. Quieter than normal, it was still a place where you could reliably be served an outstanding breakfast roll of egg and ham before dawn. At 6 a.m. on 4 September, the middle Saturday of the US Open, I walked up the street from my usual New York hotel to order one and, standing there bleary-eyed, felt a tap on the shoulder. Looming over me was the unmistakeable and very large figure of Andrew Richardson.

He had come from the opposite direction, from the Peninsula Hotel, where his stay had now lasted the best part of two weeks. Perhaps best known for its roof bar, it is not one of the five-star establishments most frequented by those who swarm in for the US Open every year. Emma Raducanu had chosen to stay away from the main player hub on Lexington, and so they were up on Fifth Avenue. One of the few familiar faces they would see there that fortnight was former prime minister Tony Blair, shadowed everywhere by his security detail.

Richardson was in good spirits, as well he might be. The trip that had begun on 24 July was now in its seventh week and was playing out far better than he or Raducanu had dared to expect. Their flights home had originally been booked for the previous Saturday, after qualifying, but they were still alive, in the third round of the US Open main draw. For the second Grand Slam in succession, she was the last British singles player of either sex still standing. That afternoon she would be playing Spain's Sara Sorribes Tormo, the world No. 41, for a place in the last sixteen.

Despite knowing that he was not likely to give too much away, I asked how it was going. 'She's playing well,' he replied with a gentle smile. Thoughts about today? 'Well, she will have her chances,' he added. Never a man to overstate things, you could detect a degree of confidence.

This was understandable enough, given that Raducanu was now on a run of five victories from what were humble and slightly unsure beginnings. She had arrived in New York fatigued from the exertions of Landisville and Chicago, and had quickly been reminded of her lowly place in the grand scheme of things at the US Open (it would have been highly irregular for the American Slam to give a young Brit a wild card). Along with most other qualifiers, she had not even been allowed to practise within the environs of Flushing Meadows on her first day. Instead, she had been exiled to the spill-over facility in neighbouring Corona Park, hitting four to a court next to the pitch-and-putt golf course sardonically known by the British media corps (who stage an annual tournament there) as Royal Flushing.

Usually players have to move through the crowds across the complex to get there, but that was not a factor this time. Spectators were banned from the qualifying event, although there was the promise of fans being allowed in on the following Monday. This was to be a three-week stretch when a lot fell into place for Raducanu, and the draw for the preliminary rounds was when the stars began aligning. She was given a Wednesday start, allowing her a much-needed extra day of rest.

The qualifying at a Grand Slam is a tournament within a tournament. There are 128 players who start, and they have to win three matches to make the main draw. The initial intake is thus whittled down to sixteen survivors, and they are then placed in the hat with 112 others for the main draw proper. In New York, her first opponent in the qualifiers would be Bibiane Schoofs, a thirty-three-year-old Dutch player ranked 283 who had played only one match since February after injury.

The day before that Raducanu did a press conference via Zoom, her first significant one since the third round at the All England Club (she had been excused duties after her traumatic fourth-round exit). Her mood was sunny enough but, reflecting on the past two months, she emphasised that there was a lot of catching-up to do: 'I think the biggest learning was how physically behind I am because I haven't done much work, relative to these other girls who have been on tour for ten years and competing,' she said. 'To be playing at the intensity that I was at for a couple weeks in a row was something completely new to me. I think that's definitely a big gap in my game. I've just been working on trying to physically get stronger and have better endurance.'

When she breezed past the overmatched Schoofs in barely an hour it completed an unusual spree for the British women. Six of them were in the qualifying and all six won – Katie Boulter, Harriet Dart, Jodie Burrage, Samantha Murray Sharan and Francesca Jones.

Their presence had seen the arrival of someone who would become a crucial part of the New York miracle – Will Herbert. A former top British junior, Herbert had learned the game in Hampstead, graduated from Loughborough University and trained as a physiotherapist after failing to make a breakthrough in the senior ranks. One of his previous clients was Alex Zverev, during the time the German was coached by Ivan Lendl. As Herbert once explained to the *Control the Controllables* podcast, that involved being subjected to the merciless humour of the one-time Czech great. After Herbert had been press-ganged into service as an emergency hitting partner for Zverev and had struggled to meet the demanding standard, the unfor-giving Lendl had forever called him 'Shank' due to a misfiring forehand. His experience of tending to top players was, however, considerable and most definitely serious. Among others he had worked with were Kyle Edmund and one-time French Open champion Ana Ivanovic.

Now he was in the employment of the Lawn Tennis Association and was a resource for those GB players at the tournament. His services were immediately in demand from Raducanu to administer running repairs on a body which had endured an unaccustomed workload for the previous fortnight. Up until then she had been relying on the duty WTA physio at the American events. Herbert later told a BBC radio documentary what he had found when first encountering her in New York: 'My memory of seeing Emma for the first time is that her body was toast. She was exhausted. She had some pretty successful weeks, so her body was a bit of a mess. Our initial aim was to get her through "qualies". That's where we felt she was.

'The mobility in her back had gone and muscles were fatigued. Our aim was to try and restore normal movement.'

The Wednesday start meant that three victories would be required in three days to qualify, and next up was Georgian left-hander Mariam Bolkvadze, the world No. 167. With the heat and humidity not far off Landisville levels, this promised to be another grind, and the dogged Georgian did not disappoint. Struggling physically in the second set on a deserted outside Court Five, and sometimes gasping for air, Raducanu trailed 5–3 in the second set and had to break back to stay in it. Somehow she summoned up the will to reel off the last four games to get safely through 6–3, 7–5.

With six British women in the preliminaries, the LTA's head of the women's game, Iain Bates, was now out in New York. He was courtside and had sensed the danger which had lurked in that second set. 'There was no doubt Emma had felt tired after Chicago,' he said. 'In that match she wanted to play quick points, but was having to work really, really hard. Bolkvadze was a break up in the second and it was a time that she really needed to dig in. She might have been a bit fatigued, but the remarkable thing about her was that it was as if she reset her mind and thought, "Right, I just need to bring my A game now and get through this," and she did.'

Strange to say, but this was the closest she came to dropping a set in the whole event. Had Bolkvadze nicked one more game in the second to test her out in a decider, the course of history might well have been changed.

The third examination looked likely to be the toughest, and with good reason. The opponent was the fourth qualifying seed, Egypt's Mayar Sherif, already a top-100 player and ranked 55 places higher. Earlier in the month she had made the final of a main-tour WTA event in Romania, and was one of the circuit's fastest risers. This reckoned without a display of serving from Raducanu that made a nonsense of any differential. Landing nearly 80 per cent of her first deliveries in, the Kent teenager faced only one break point and the seventy-three-minute duration of the 6–1, 6–4 victory meant the heat never became a factor. Qualification had been achieved, alongside two other British women in Boulter and Dart.

That night called for a celebration and Raducanu took Richardson and her agent, Chris Helliar, to the Strip House which, while sounding salacious, is nothing more than one of New York's best-known steak restaurants. There was more good news in that the draw had placed her in the half which would be starting on the Tuesday, meaning there was the relative luxury of having three blank days to rest and recuperate.

The British player was now in a cycle where she was improving with every match. That weekend she sat down with Richardson, who two weeks later reflected on their conversation: 'She had beaten the fourth [qualifying] seed and managed to come through that,' he recalled. 'I could see that Emma's level was extremely high. She had started to gain confidence in Chicago and Landisville. I said, "It is going to take a really good performance to beat you. If you keep performing the way you're performing, someone's going to have to play really well to win."'

By now Tim Henman had arrived in town, as part of the much slimmed-down broadcasting team which had been sent by Amazon Prime, the UK TV rights holders for the tournament. While most of their regulars were back in London due to the restrictions in numbers of those allowed on site, it was another twist of fate that he was one of the few who made it out there. Henman's experience extended to three times making the second week at Flushing Meadows, including one semi-final appearance. He was to prove a valuable sounding board (and regular dinner companion) for his old friend Richardson as the path was plotted through the draw.

The first day of any Grand Slam is a frantic affair, and what was to go down as one of the greatest tennis tournaments of all time (not just because of Raducanu) began with a different British player dominating the agenda. Metal hip or not, Andy Murray had refused to be written out of the story and on 30 August 2021 he played his part in a remarkable five-set match which ended in a narrow defeat to third seed Stefanos Tsitsipas. A tournament which would climax with Emma Raducanu's name on everyone's lips began with a strange theme: what the Americans would term 'going to the bathroom'. Murray was furious at the length of the off-court break the Greek took at the end of the fourth set, and the topic of visits to the loo became the issue du jour.

The initial Monday also brought the news that another British No. 1 who had achieved so much, Jo Konta, was pulling out due to more of the knee problems that would contribute to the ending of her career later in the year. While Raducanu could sit out the opening day there was, however, a significant development. Her scheduled first-round opponent, the previous year's semi-finalist and thirteenth seed, Jennifer Brady, announced she was withdrawing due to a foot injury. The replacement would be Switzerland's **Stefanie Voegele**. She was classed as a 'lucky loser'. This refers to someone who has perished in the final round of qualifying, but is of high enough rank to head the queue to replace any last-minute dropouts. It was billed as another good break for Raducanu. However, given that the American Brady had no form after playing only three matches since the French Open, thanks to her ongoing foot difficulties, she would have been ripe for an upset.

A consequence of her withdrawal was a court reshuffle. While the original match featuring an American had been slated for the huge Louis Armstrong Stadium, the match between a British qualifier and a Swiss lucky loser was relegated to the smaller Court 17. This is the sunken arena which has become known as 'The Pit', and it would host two of Raducanu's matches before she began hitting the big time on Arthur Ashe.

Voegele, once a top-fifty player despite a quirky service motion, began the match as if she was playing with house money, as if she had been reprieved. She fired some carefree early winners to go an early break up, but after that Raducanu picked up where she had left off the previous Friday. Soon she was in the ascendancy, with her first-serve percentage touching 80 once again. The one kink in her performance came when trying to close it out. Six match points came and went before she forced an error from the Swiss to seal it on number seven. 'Everyone could tell I was getting a bit shaky at the end. I was so relieved to finish it off', she admitted, smiling.

The reward was a second round with **Zhang Shuai**, the Chinese No. 1 who had given her something of a schooling in San Jose at the start of the trip. It was when looking ahead to this match that we discovered something new about Raducanu – her linguistic skills. Some players do so many press conferences that you soon cease learning much that is fresh about their background, but the fact was that at this point the eighteen-year-old had been relatively unexposed. Revealing a bond with her next opponent through their chats in the locker room, she nonchalantly added, 'I'd say my Mandarin is decent. I speak to my mum quite a bit in Mandarin. I can't read or write it, but it's great because when we're at home, I can speak to my mum in it when I don't want my dad to understand, so it's like our secret language. And it also helps because some of the Chinese players are very nice and friendly.'

Since the two of them had faced each other in early August Raducanu had played fourteen matches and won twelve of them. The Chinese player was about to discover the improvement this had brought about. The night before had seen a biblical storm in New York, with dramatic pictures emerging of the rain sheeting into the supposedly indoor Louis Armstrong Stadium through ventilation gaps. A giant mopping-up operation was in full swing across the city, roads were blocked and the British player and her small team had to make an early start to reach Queens: 'It took us about ninety minutes to get in and it was a bit of a rush to the warm-ups. We knew something would happen after last night and I just hope everyone is safe,' she said later.

The disrupted preparation had not put her off her stride. She broke to love in the first game, showcasing the startling improvement that had come about in recent weeks. The ball was taken early, returns were mercilessly driven back from an offensive position. The experienced top-fifty player was helpless and, if anything, the 6–2 first-set scoreline understated its one-sided nature. Raducanu drove on to 4–0 in the second before Zhang began to show some resistance, fighting back to 4–5. Playing on Court 10, which backs onto Corona Park, the British player came out to serve for the match just as a marching band was going past. Horns and drums were blaring on the other side of the large hedge which borders the court. She tried to turn that into a positive: 'I sort of twisted my mind into thinking they were supporting me, so actually that helped me at the end,' said Raducanu after wrapping up another straight-sets victory.

Counting back through qualifying, she had now won two more matches in New York than at Wimbledon – it was as if the show had successfully transferred from the West End to Broadway.

The middle Saturday at Flushing Meadows always heralds the start of Labor Day weekend. The city can be eerily quiet compared to normal, although in 2021 those few days felt much like any others of the time. Such was the dampening effect, on Midtown at least, of the pandemic's stubborn refusal to dissipate. The crowds were still turning out for the tennis, albeit in slightly diminished numbers, as Raducanu prepared to meet **Sara Sorribes Tormo** in the third round.

This promised to be her sternest test to date, against someone straight out of Spanish tennis's central casting unit. Sorribes Tormo comes from the Valencia region, like David Ferrer, the recently retired top-five men's player, and that was not the only thing they had in common. It is a compliment to say that she had acquired a similar reputation for scrapping for every point from the baseline, forcing the opponent to play an extra ball and acting as the proverbial human brick wall. This method had already brought her twenty-nine victories on tour that season, including one at the Tokyo Olympics against Ash Barty.

When the two players walked out on Court 17 the stadium was respectably half full, although that made one newspaper's breathless assertion that Emma mania was already sweeping the United States look a tad exaggerated. What followed was little short of sensational. This was the match that made those

Above: Tim Henman, working at the 2021 US Open for Amazon Prime, was an invaluable source of support and advice throughout the tournament.

Left: Raducanu's natural rapport with the crowd grew ever stronger as she progressed through the rounds at Flushing Meadows.

Below: The hard work on her American tour pays off as she beats Chinese No. 1 Zhang Shuai in the second round in New York, avenging her loss in San Jose the previous month.

Raducanu's 6–0, 6–1 defeat of Spain's Sara Sorribes Tormo in the third round was an almost flawless display.

'She absolutely capitalised on the moment' – though unhappy with her own losing performance in front of her home crowd, Shelby Rogers was generous about her fourth-round opponent.

On the way to victory over Olympic gold medallist Belinda Bencic in the quarter-final – displaying the athleticism and determination that helped her sweep through the tournament without losing a set

Left: Making light of the late-evening start, Raducanu hits a powerful return as she races to a 5–0 lead against her semi-final opponent, Greece's Maria Sakkari.

Above: The fairy tale continues – in the on-court interview, her reaction to becoming the first ever qualifier, male or female, to reach a Grand Slam final is infectious.

Below: To mark the twentieth anniversary of 9/11, a giant flag is unfurled in the Arthur Ashe Stadium before two teenagers, Raducanu and Canadian Leylah Fernandez, contest the 2021 US Open final.

Undaunted by the scale of the occasion, she starts the final with remarkable assurance, claiming the first set 6–4.

Her 'lucky charm' – Virginia Wade (*left*), Britain's last women's Grand Slam winner, likes what she sees as Raducanu's impressive form continues in the final.

Coach Andrew Richardson (*left*), physiotherapist Will Herbert (*right*) and other members of the British support team have plenty to celebrate.

At a crucial point in the second set, Raducanu keeps her cool as her bleeding knee is dressed while Leylah Fernandez expresses her frustration to WTA Supervisor Clare Wood.

Above: By 6.10 p.m. Emma Raducanu had earned the opportunity to serve for the championship.

Right: 'How's that for an ending?' asks commentator Mary Carillo as Raducanu falls to the floor after the winning ace.

Below: Tennis's newest star proudly receives the trophy from one of the all-time greats, America's Billie Jean King.

Dress from Chanel, jewellery from Tiffany's, the new champion attends the Met Gala in New York two days after the final.

Back in Britain, recognition of her achievements included the BBC Sports Personality of the Year award in December 2021.

Clare Balding (*centre*) helps the LTA celebrate the homecoming of an unprecedented four British US Open champions: (*left to right*) Gordon Reid and Alfie Hewett (men's wheelchair doubles), Emma Raducanu and Joe Salisbury (men's doubles).

With public expectations high, early defeat in her first post-US Open tournament, at Indian Wells, brought some harsh criticism, but Raducanu kept things in perspective: 'This is going to be very small in the long term.'

At the Transylvania Open in October 2021, Elena-Gabriela Ruse (*left*) and the other host-nation players were impressed by Raducanu's grasp of Romanian.

Raducanu battles to an impressive win against America's Sloane Stephens in the 2022 Australian Open, but frustrating blisters prevent further progress.

of us who saw it sit bolt upright. It became clearer why Richardson, nine hours earlier in the corner deli, had sounded suspiciously understated when he suggested that his player might have her chances.

She proceeded to utterly obliterate her world-ranked-41 opponent with an almost flawless display. Taking the heavily spun ball coming at her on the rise, Raducanu pumped winner after winner into the corners, leaving Sorribes Tormo flailing at thin air. After a ten-minute second game it was over in the blink of an eye and a drop of the jaw. The Kent teenager had a match point to deliver the dreaded 'double bagel' (6–0, 6–0), and it was noticeable that she was cross with herself for not doing so.

After settling for 6–0, 6–1, the rewards and records were beginning to stack up. The win meant a guaranteed break into the top 100 and £190,000 in prize money. She had become the first player since Jennifer Capriati, thirty-one years previously, to make the last sixteen at her first two Grand Slams. The courtside Iain Bates was among those needing to catch his breath.

'That was a mind-blowing performance,' he said, looking back some months later. 'At that point, I'm not thinking she's going to go on and win the US Open, but then you think who else would have done that nearly love and love? Emma was just striking it into the corners, taking the ball out of the air, serving so powerfully. It was one of those matches you sat at the side pinching yourself. Just reaching the fourth round of the US Open to repeat what she had done at Wimbledon was amazing for an eighteen-year-old.'

Back at the media compound Tim Henman was preparing to give his thoughts to camera. Before doing so he puffed out his cheeks in near disbelief: 'I'm reluctant to contribute to people getting carried away, but the truth is it was phenomenal,' he admitted. 'I couldn't have been more impressed. Emma is already technically very tight and solid. Of course improvements can be made, but you really don't need to change much there.'

Now, for the first time that fortnight, Raducanu was summoned into the main interview room to be questioned in person by the media. Incredibly, this was the first time she had ever been in that situation, as reporters had been kept entirely separate at Wimbledon because of the pandemic and 'bubble' restrictions. Not that it was especially intimidating in an auditorium that can normally fit around 200. With attendance limited to a smattering of Americans and a vastly reduced international corps, it rarely got beyond a tenth full. The low-key nature of those gatherings may have been another helpful factor in the fortnight. There was certainly nothing like the surreal occurrence of 2012 in the same room, when Andy Murray's press conference was gatecrashed by two slightly tipsy Scottish knights of the realm, Sir Alex Ferguson and Sir Sean Connery, along with his mother Judy. (Not that it put him off, as he proceeded to win the tournament.)

Raducanu seemed to quite enjoy the experience, but largely restricted herself to a measured and unarguable analysis of the reasons behind a startling performance: 'I think I'm playing better tennis here than at Wimbledon,' she said. 'Of course being on the hard courts, they're less forgiving than grass. But honestly I think with the amount of matches I have played and the experience that I have accumulated in the last four, five weeks, my game is just getting better with each match.'

There was more good news that Saturday night when she discovered that her next opponent would be American Shelby Rogers, and not Ash Barty. Having been on the road since March, Barty, the Wimbledon champion, looked slightly weary and was edged out in a third-set tiebreak. That meant it was the world No. 43, and not the world No. 1, who lay in store at the start of week two.

Something more subtle was happening that weekend, which also played into Raducanu's hands. With Roger Federer, Rafael Nadal, men's champion Dominic Thiem and Serena Williams all absent, the tournament was already in short supply of legends. There had been two major third-round upsets by teen-agers – Spaniard Carlos Alcaraz beating Tsitsipas and Leylah Fernandez taking down Naomi Osaka. Suddenly a theme was emerging of a new generation breaking through to rattle the more established order, and it permeated through all the media and TV coverage. Try as they might to insulate themselves, players cannot entirely escape it when this kind of vibe takes hold, partly because it starts to come up in most press confer-ences. When draws open up it can unnerve some players, and that is what happened.

American Frances Tiafoe, also into the fourth round, was especially graphic about it when asked about the atmosphere in the locker rooms with the big beasts absent: 'You don't have Roger, Rafa. Guys are hungry, guys are like, "It's the f****** Open, I got to f****** push!"' he said. 'So I think that has definitely a part to play in it. Anyone can beat anyone. You have qualifiers in the round of sixteen. Everyone's good. If you don't show up to play, you can lose to anyone. I definitely think guys are trying extra hard. I see guys foaming in the mouth. It's pretty funny to watch. I'm in the locker room cracking up.'

The US media was now definitely taking note of Raducanu, and for the Labor Day Monday (a public holiday) she was placed on the Arthur Ashe Stadium. Built in 1997 and named after the great player and humanitarian, it holds just shy of 24,000 spectators, the same as a decent-sized football stadium. While obviously smaller than a soccer field, the whole playing area is nonetheless unusually large outside the lines. That, combined with the massive banks of seats around it in three sections, makes the visuals completely different for those unfamiliar. Andrew Richardson asked Tim Henman to have an informal chat with his player about what to look out for and what could be different, as it was sure to take some adjusting. As it happened, Andy Murray had discussed the same topic with Raducanu before the tournament.

Shelby Rogers, her opponent, had played on Arthur Ashe the round before, which was an advantage, but she was not without pressure herself. Despite not being among her country's best-known players, she was the host nation's last female singles player standing, as Raducanu had been at the same stage of Wimbledon.

British tennis royalty came to watch in the form of Virginia Wade. She had also once been based in Kent, but in the 1970s chose to live mainly in New York, partly to escape the 83 per cent top rate of tax in the UK at the time. Having been unable to make her usual summer visit to Wimbledon because of travel restrictions, she was now keen to see what the fuss was about.

If Wade was royalty, then the young pretender turned in a command performance, although it has to be said that Rogers unexpectedly crumbled after an impressive start. The American went 2–0 up as the Arthur Ashe debutante adjusted to the new sightlines. Two games was all that took as, having saved two break points at 0–2, 15–40, Raducanu reeled off eleven straight games for the second match in succession. The initial power of Rogers was defused, and by the second set she was littering the court with errors as she pressed too hard. It was all over in sixty-six minutes and again it was striking how the British player's momentum was unstoppable once she began hitting with freedom. The Raducanu Roll was becoming a thing.

Notably, the young player had the presence of mind and good manners during the immediate on-court interview to thank 1968 US Open champion Wade for coming, describing her as 'an absolute legend'. Outside the stadium afterwards, before slipping away to her home on Long Island, the heroine of the Silver Jubilee Wimbledon in 1977 stopped to chat, making clear her admiration for what she had just witnessed: 'Emma ticks all the boxes. She's got good concentration, great groundstrokes, her serve was awesome, and she knows what to do with the ball. I think probably the way she concentrates so well and her determination is maybe the best feature of all. But everything else is good as well. The serve is very consistent, technically very sound.

'I would like to see her look to come forward more because that would make the difference. But she has a very bright future, I think she's better than [2019 champion Bianca] Andreescu, for example. She's still got some physical development to do. Around twenty she will be okay. You have to pace yourself. I will be back on Wednesday. Hopefully I'll be a lucky charm.'

The crestfallen Rogers would become the first player of that week to chide herself after facing the newcomer: 'That was pretty embarrassing,' the American bluntly admitted. 'It took everything I had to beat Barty. I guess that was a little apparent today.'

Rogers is also known as one of the more generous personalities on the tour, and while her self-analysis was lacerating, she was also complimentary about her opponent: 'She's on Arthur Ashe Stadium for the first time, there's a lot of challenges for her,' said Rogers. 'So she did handle that very well. She absolutely capitalised on the moment.'

Raducanu herself admitted amazement at what was happening, and was delighted by the way she had adjusted to a very new playing environment: 'Personally, I am surprised that I'm here,' she said. 'I didn't expect it – I knew I was doing a lot of great work that would pay off someday, but you never know when. Being here in the US Open quarter-finals, after not playing for eighteen months, is absolutely incredible.'

She was speaking as someone who had lost fewer games, fifteen, in the first four rounds than any player in New York since Serena Williams in 2013.

*   *   *

The narrative of this being a big fortnight for teenagers was now the talk of the town. Carlos Alcaraz in the men's and Leylah Fernandez in the women's had also won and added to the youthful representation in the last eight of the singles. The Canadian Fernandez had turned nineteen at the start of the week, and she celebrated by handing out cupcakes in the locker room. Another theme gaining currency was that, after tennis had been through so many struggles in 2021, this was turning out to be one of the most exciting tournaments in memory, for both sexes. On the men's side, for example, thirty-three matches in the first seven days had gone to five sets. Ten of them had seen wins coming back from two sets to love down.

Amid all this, Raducanu was trying to stay aloof from the gathering mania. She was content to remain in her room, hermit-like, ordering in food every evening. The only concession to altering the hotel-courts-practice-play cycle through the fortnight was the odd walk down to Times Square to buy frozen yoghurt.

'I have been focusing one day at a time, taking care of each day,' she said. 'When you're playing tournaments, you get into this sort of autopilot mode of your routines, recovering on the day off in between.'

Her next opponent, as the midday match on Arthur Ashe on Wednesday, 8 September, was **Belinda Bencic**. The Swiss player had been an outstanding teenager who had never quite delivered on her initial promise, but that process now looked as if it was beginning to happen. She had won the Olympic gold medal in Tokyo and was hoping that it would have the same effect as it once had on Andy Murray. The Scot always felt that his success at London 2012 was a key stepping stone to him winning his first Grand Slam at Flushing Meadows barely a month later.

After four games of the quarter-final it very much looked like this was where the fairy tale for the young British player would end. Bencic, who had seen off another young challenger in Iga Świątek the previous round, surged to a 3–1 lead. Raducanu was struggling to adjust to the weight of ball coming from the other end and her range was off. Then came yet another dramatic turnaround as she reeled off five straight games to take the set. Bencic was starting to take on the bemused look of previous opponents.

The Swiss had only had her serve broken three times in the four rounds before, and that tally would double as she was beaten 6–3, 6–4. This said a lot about how good the Raducanu return of serve had become, shaping up to be one of the outstanding shots in the women's game. As with the great batters in cricket, it comes from seeing the ball early, being able to read the motion of your opponent (bowler/server) and then having the agility and hand-eye to react in a split second. And once again Raducanu showed remarkable sangfroid when the world No. 11 threatened to assert her quality towards the end. At 4–3 and 5–4 when serving, the Kent teenager was reduced to 0–30 down both times, but was able then to produce the deliveries that would get herself out of trouble.

After eighty-two minutes she became the first qualifier in the modern era to have reached the US Open semi-finals. The player herself was oblivious: 'I have actually got no idea about any of the records at all. It was the first time I heard today that

I was the first qualifier to make the semis. I had no idea before that,' she said. 'I'm not here to chase any records right now. I'm just taking care of what I can do in the moment. I haven't even started thinking about the next one yet.'

Raducanu's self-assurance in press conferences and in TV interviews was drawing purrs of admiration from international all comers in the media. Perhaps it was her education, certainly her upbringing, maybe being an only child helped in that she would have spent a lot of time around adults, but she was handling it all like a veteran. There was even the odd lyrical flourish about where she found herself: 'I think to compare yourself and your results against anyone is probably the thief of happiness,' was one quote she threw in after the Bencic match.

With interest spreading far beyond the realm of sport – and the online departments of publications beginning to register record-breaking clicks on any story containing her name – every aspect of this run was attracting attention. One of those was the enforced absence of her parents, who could not enter the United States. 'It's not possible, because you need a waiver and it takes a couple weeks for approval. It's too late, and they won't be able to get one,' explained Raducanu, before laughing about a couple of messages home going unanswered. 'I haven't actually called my parents for quite a while. Yesterday they were ghosting me, but when we speak it's more just, because I have been away for so long now, they just really want to see how I am. I think right now I've got such a great support team around me, a tight-knit group of people that I really trust, and they are really helping me through these moments.'

She also divulged what had surprised her the most from a technical standpoint about a run that had seen her win eight matches without dropping a set. This included a Novak Djokovic-style ability to skid across the hard courts, something he partly attributes to a childhood spent skiing. 'I'd say one of the things is my movement. Physically I would say I'm not 100 per cent developed yet, but my speed and ability to get to some of the balls has definitely surprised me,' reflected Raducanu. 'I have started sliding, which I didn't know I could do actually, and I kind of do it by accident now. I have always wanted to learn how, but now it seems I can.'

Later on, her semi-final opponent was decided when Greece's **Maria Sakkari** continued her career-best year by taking down fourth seed Karolína Plíšková 6–4, 6–4. This was another small factor in the great star alignment. The towering Czech can take a match away from anyone with her enormous serve, but it looked like she had blinked when confronted with this chance to break her Grand Slam duck, having lost in the Wimbledon final. Sakkari was a strong baseliner, but the type of player you are at least going to get into the rallies against. In the other semi-final Fernandez was playing another who can take a match away with her sheer power, the second seed Aryna Sabalenka of Belarus.

Around 6 p.m. on that second Thursday, 9 September, I ventured out onto the deserted Arthur Ashe to watch Raducanu's preparatory hit before the double bill of the women's semis. Iain Bates was standing mid-court, firing down serves to warm up her returns. As a very tall left-hander, Andrew Richardson could not replicate what would be coming at her later. It was notable that the young British player seemed not to have a care, smiling and joking with her small team.

She would have a long wait thereafter. The brave Fernandez began the evening by taking yet another major scalp in Sabalenka, edging through a deciding set 6–4. Then came a lengthy on-court presentation to the 'Original Nine'. These were the pioneers of women's tennis who, under the leadership of Billie Jean King, had stepped up to form the women's tour as its own entity, fifty years previously.

It was 10.17 p.m., the middle of the night back in the UK, when Raducanu walked out for another of those rare outings under lights. Those who got up or stayed up to watch were rewarded with another performance of remarkable maturity. A 6–1, 6–4 score if anything understated the dominance of the younger player. Having saved three break points in the first game, the teenager raced to a 5–0 lead before the world No. 17 got on the board. So resilient was Raducanu's second serve that she was winning three out of four points when it was required – a very high mark in top-level tennis. She relentlessly attacked her opponent's weaker forehand side.

With the clock ticking closer to midnight, the muscular Sakkari eventually started to show why she was normally such a formidable competitor, but it was too late. Serving with new balls to close out the match, Raducanu dropped the first point before winning the next four to seal it at the first time of asking. The New York crowd, who had stayed out late in impressive numbers, roared its approval.

She was now the first ever qualifier, anywhere, male or female, to make a Grand Slam final. A minimum sum of £900,000 had been banked. The US Open had its first all-teenage final since 1999. In the immediate on-court stadium interview Raducanu was asked how she would handle it. 'Is there any expectation?' she replied jokingly. 'I'm a qualifier, so there's no pressure on me!'

Thursday was well into Friday by the time she came in to fulfil her last media commitments. Asked how she would describe her feat, she replied, 'A surprise. Honestly I just can't believe it. A shock. Crazy. All of the above. I never really realised that I would take tennis as a career until maybe two years ago. I always had dreams of playing in Grand Slams, but I just didn't know when they would come. To come this early, at this point in my career . . . I've only really been on tour for a month, two months since Wimbledon. It's pretty crazy to me.'

For her part, Sakkari was devastated that she would not be the one getting a crack at Leylah Fernandez to win a Grand Slam title. Like Shelby Rogers, she was known to be one of the more generous characters in the locker room, and she provided a similarly interesting commentary on what had happened in the quarter- and semi-finals. Again, there was the strong hint that the more experienced players, seeing a path towards Grand Slam glory, had baulked at it in the face of a challenge from a younger player.

Of Raducanu she said, 'She plays fearless. She absolutely goes for it. She does the right thing, actually. She has nothing to lose. She's enjoying herself. But we were all absent from the court these days playing against her. I saw Belinda yesterday. I don't want to speak for her, but I think she would agree with me that we did not bring our best performance. I'm sad. I'm very broken that I couldn't make it to my first final.'

Before leaving the stadium in the early hours, her media duties done, Raducanu wanted to do one more thing. She and Chris Helliar went back into the deserted Arthur Ashe Stadium, the lights dimmed and with everyone gone home, and took a moment to sit in the stands and contemplate, taking it all in. After nine matches, and nine wins in fifteen days, there was one more challenge to come in the great adventure.

With the precious trophy after an astonishing performance in the final.

8

THE FINAL

The sun rose over Manhattan on 11 September 2021 and, just like the corresponding day twenty years previously, there was barely a cloud in the sky. Of course this was no ordinary morning in New York, and on this date it never will be again. Not after the attacks on the Twin Towers of 2001 which have shaped the modern history of this city. Around Midtown there were banners hung from lamp posts commemorating what happened, and on the streets the passers-by were mainly either in uniform or in suits, going to and from events to mark the occasion. Around the corner from Emma Raducanu's Fifth Avenue hotel was parked a fire engine, with the names of 344 personnel who lost their lives in the rescue effort listed on the side. Just down from there, off Lexington Avenue, around 200 people were gathered on 51st Street, outside its fire station, for a service remembering those who died.

Tennis seems an even more trivial pursuit than usual in this context but, within the parish of that sport, big things were happening later in the day. They would involve two young women who were not even born when the 2001 atrocity took place. At 4 p.m. Raducanu would be reacquainting herself with Leylah Fernandez, the nineteen-year-old Canadian she had first met at the Under-12s of the Orange Bowl, and then in the Wimbledon juniors. That the final would be contested by two teenagers ranked 150 and 73 only added to the fascination. Moreover, they had other things in common. Both had strong connections to Toronto (Raducanu was born in the city, while Fernandez was born in Quebec before growing up there) and were of mixed heritage. For her part, Fernandez was the daughter of a former footballer from Ecuador and a mother originally from the Philippines. Raducanu, with her Romanian-Chinese roots, had left Canada aged two. There were an unusual number of territories with a proxy interest in the outcome of this final.

The day before, Jorge Fernandez – who like Ian Raducanu had supervised his talented offspring's tennis development – had given a powerful and emotional interview to TSN in Canada. In it he expressed his gratitude to his adopted country for helping provide his family with opportunities. 'There's a lot of talk in the news about, you know, immigrant people,' he said. 'And I understand nationalist sentiments and I understand how we need to protect and we only have so many resources. I understand all of that and I don't want to get political; that's not what I'm doing. What I'm telling you is that we're an immigrant family, and we had nothing. Got in with nothing. So, Canada opened up its doors, and if they wouldn't have done what they did, I wouldn't have had the opportunities that I have, and I wouldn't have been able to give them to my daughter. That's it, so, it means a lot.' This was the latest step on what had been a difficult journey. His daughter had told of how for three years during her childhood her mother had spent most of the time working away from the family home, sometimes in California, to help finance the talented offspring's tennis development.

In more prosaic tennis terms, the significant backdrop to the final was the contrasting route the two players had taken. Fernandez had needed to play six matches, and had beaten three of the world's top five in Aryna Sabalenka, Naomi Osaka and Elina Svitolina. Raducanu had not faced anyone higher than world No. 11 Bencic, but as a qualifier had played nine rounds. Despite that, she had spent seventy fewer minutes on the court in reaching the championship match. So who would be in better stead: the battle-hardened Fernandez who had come through so many scrapes against the best players in the world, or the rookie for whom winning had become a reflexive action, albeit not against anyone from the top ten? Raducanu's biggest final had been in Chicago, before a few hundred people, while Fernandez was certainly further advanced on her tennis journey. She had already won a WTA main tour event earlier in the season, in Mexico.

The flowing left-hander was part of an unlikely surge in Canadian tennis that had already seen success for the likes of Milos Raonic, Eugenie Bouchard, Bianca Andreescu, Félix Auger-Aliassime and Denis Shapovalov. The country had produced six Grand Slam singles semi-finalists since 2014. Fernandez had jokingly put this down to the maple syrup – and what other reason could there be? Perhaps it could be connected to the large inflow of families originally from Eastern Europe. The parents of Andreescu, the 2019 US champion, had made the same journey from Romania as Ian Raducanu once did, although it does not appear that their paths had crossed.

If an omen was being sought for the Brits that Saturday, it was provided by three GB men who were part of the curtain-raiser for the main action of the day. Starting at 1 p.m on the Arthur Ashe Stadium, Londoner Joe Salisbury had followed up his triumph in the men's doubles (winning the previous day, with Rajeev Ram, against Jamie Murray and Bruno Soares) with victory in the mixed final, alongside American Desirae Krawczyk. Simultaneously, in the men's wheelchair final on the Louis Armstrong Stadium, Alfie Hewett and Gordon Reid were beating Gustavo Fernández and Shingo Kunieda 6–2, 6–1.

As Iain Bates – now close to the end of an unexpectedly long stay – pointed out, other players from the UK doing well deep into the tournament certainly did no harm: 'It's always good to have other Brits around. Joe and Jamie were about and we had the wheelchair players going great. There were still a lot of British faces around the corridors on that final weekend. That was an important presence throughout the three weeks. There was a nice camaraderie, but I think Emma does what Emma does, irrespective of how many others are there. She had to do what she can in her own way.'

It was true she could not afford to get distracted by events elsewhere, and staying in a regular routine was essential. Bates was also in something of a pattern, although he got a surprise after rising for his morning exercise: 'I went out to go for my usual run and the first thing I came across was the police barricades as Joe Biden was staying in the hotel opposite. Other than that, everyone would know that sticking to the normal day-to-day routine is important.'

There was something inevitably different in the warm-up sessions out at Flushing Meadows, however. Crowds were thronging to watch Raducanu on the main stretch of practice courts at the complex that have stands behind them.

'Emma warmed up right in front of the ESPN studio at the far end,' recalls Bates. 'I was there with Flex [Richardson], and he was hitting with her because he's left-handed like Fernandez. Chris [Helliar] and Will [Herbert] and Tim [Henman] were at the side watching. There were far more people watching her practising than for Daniil Medvedev on the next court, and he was playing in the men's final. That was just the magnitude the story had got to around them. But to be honest, none of us were really quite aware of all that until we got home.'

Expectation had reached such a pitch that good-luck messages were flowing in from all quarters. 'The whole country will be cheering you on in the final,' Boris Johnson posted. This was added to by the Duke and Duchess of Cambridge. Canadian prime minister Justin Trudeau weighed in too.

Certainly the central British character in this drama was unaware of the machinations going on around television coverage back in the UK. At the eleventh hour Amazon Prime Video decided to share the rights with Channel 4 for the sum of £1 million in a one-off deal which would ensure the final reached a much bigger audience. In excess of 10 million, it turned out, was estimated to be the case. It meant that, back home, more parties and weddings that Saturday night would see large groups distracted as they gathered around televisions and mobile phones. More pub screens would be surrounded in a way that would be usually associated with football.

Raducanu stuck to her normal pre-match rituals: practise, eat, stretch, go through the game plan. Tennis is a simple game to the untrained eye, and essentially that is true, but at the highest level tactical preparations are a big part, an area that the Kent teenager is particularly attuned to. Throughout the tournament, Andrew Richardson had not been afraid to consult the likes of Mark Petchey, Tim Henman and Jeremy Bates for their thoughts before passing his final assessments on to his player. There are a multitude of aspects to be assessed, as players tend to have established patterns of play which they prefer. For example, what type of serve does your opponent hit when under the most pressure? Which stroke is most likely to break down? From what area of the court do they like to pull the trigger and go for an outright winner? For this match, an instance of one key battleground was likely to be the Canadian's swinging left-handed serve into the British player's backhand return.

*　　*　　*

When the hour came ahead of the 4 p.m. start, the Arthur Ashe Stadium was already nearly full. The pageantry of American sports leans heavily towards the military, and at Flushing Meadows the national anthem is sung and soldiers unfurl a giant Stars and Stripes flag across the court. The players entered the arena, with Fernandez getting the slightly louder roar.

The Canadian's player box was full, one of its occupants being her most prominent celebrity supporter, former NBA star and compatriot Steve Nash. The familiar faces for Raducanu were her coach Richardson, physio Will Herbert, agent Chris Helliar and the LTA's Iain Bates. Perhaps helpfully, Tim Henman was even closer to the court, seated in his broadcast position in the sunken photographers' area behind advertising hoardings.

The atmosphere for the first all-teenage final since 1999, when Serena Williams had defeated Martina Hingis, was little short of febrile. After so much struggle and darkness around tennis in the previous eighteen months, there was a sense that this was the sport breaking back into the light.

From the outset it was clear that neither player was going to be cowed by the scale of the occasion and the biggest crowd in tennis, although it was Raducanu who started the more assured. She held with relative ease in the opener before a 16-point second game ensued. At the sixth time of asking, the eighteen-year-old British player took a break point when Fernandez skewed a forehand. Twenty-three minutes had gone when the Canadian broke back for 1–2 when Raducanu slapped a backhand into the net on a fourth break point.

By the ninth game it was still even, although the Fernandez serve had looked the shakier of the two. At 5–4 Raducanu struck the first decisive blow. She earned herself three set points, only for all to be missed through a backhand sent long, a miscued lob and a backhand return fired into the net. Back at deuce, she forced a fourth, with an inside-out forehand that screamed into the far corner. Then came a forehand winner down the line, delivered from a crouched position, to claim the set 6–4. In the moment, Raducanu whirled her arms around once to turn up the volume from all corners of the vast stadium.

There had been little in it, although Raducanu had won 48 per cent of her return points, compared to the 40 per cent of her opponent. Overall she had won 43 points to 38.

Early in the second set came the first, and only, momentum shift towards Fernandez. From 0–40 down in the second game she won five straight points and then broke serve herself to lead 2–1. Raducanu immediately responded by levelling when she attacked a string of second serves with her backhand. After holding for 3–2, she got to 40–30 against the Fernandez serve and scrambled back a return just over the net, more in hope than expectation. The Canadian had time to think about where to put the high ball away. Whether by instinct, guess-work or both, Raducanu picked the right side and when the ball was directed straight into her wheelhouse – preferred strike zone – she fired a forehand back down the line for a blistering winner.

At 5–2 she was a game away from glory and then, twice, just a point away. Only then did she exhibit signs of nerves, anxiously putting a backhand wide and, on the second match point, sending a forehand into the net. Fernandez held, thereby asking the question of whether her opponent could serve it out at 5–3. Points were traded to get to 30-all and the next one was dictated by the Canadian. In the course of losing it, while chasing behind the baseline, Raducanu lost her footing and scraped her knee along the concrete surface. Seeing blood seeping from the wound, she calmly walked to her chair to seek attention.

The physio was summoned to the court by umpire Marijana Veljović, and Fernandez was unhappy at the hiatus. WTA Supervisor Clare Wood walked onto the court to hear the waiting player's protests while the wound was dressed and the long streak of blood down the Raducanu shin was cleaned up. Fernandez told her that she had suffered a cut in an early round that fortnight but the match had not been stopped. Wood, a former British No. 1 and a hugely experienced official, calmly explained that blood injuries should always be met with immediate treatment. A later study of the rulebook proved her entirely correct.

Five minutes and five seconds had passed by the time Raducanu served again, and she nervelessly came off better from an eight-shot rally. With Veljović appealing for calm among the crowd, Fernandez then played a brilliant defensive lob to keep the next point alive. Six strokes later, Raducanu attempted a winner but sent the forehand long, which created another break opportunity. That was saved with a stretched overhead that came off the edge of the British player's strings, pulling it back to deuce. Match point came again when a rasping backhand down the line forced Fernandez to hit long with the attempted reply.

As destiny called, Raducanu took her time. She went to her towel, briefly rubbed down, returned to her mark and threw the ball up against the New York sky. Down came the racket with a relatively open face, sending the ball straight and true into the corner, flying way beyond the reach of Fernandez. The Arthur Ashe Stadium erupted for the final time. As Raducanu said later: 'I don't think I made one serve that wide in the whole match, to be honest. I was like, "If I'm going to make it, this is going to be the time." I drove my legs up to that ball-toss like never before. I landed it.'

It was just shy of 6.10 p.m. and it felt like all the clocks had stopped. The miracle of New York was complete, 112 days after she had suffered that first loss at Essex's Connaught Club following her A-levels. 'How's that for an ending?' asked esteemed American commentator Mary Carillo on the TV commentary, in an almost stunned sotto voce. 'She went ten rounds without dropping a set.'

The victor fell to the floor, lying on her back with her hands covering her face. The loser sportingly walked round the net to meet her and embrace. Amid the cacophony Raducanu asked Veljović if she could leave the court to give her small team a celebratory hug up in the box – as if she would refuse. Now she was walking in the same shoes as the greats, like the watching Martina Navratilova, Chris Evert and Monica Seles.

Back on the court, amid swirling ticker tape, Billie Jean King presented her with the trophy and a cheque worth £1.8 million. A measure of her astonishing progress was that this represented more than seven times her previous career prize money, the lion's share of which had come from one tournament,

Wimbledon. The youngest Grand Slam-winner since Maria Sharapova at Wimbledon in 2004 said all the right things at the presentation ceremony, as did Fernandez. The Canadian's final words into the microphone were particularly resonant, and emphasised that she had been one half of a superb final between two mightily impressive teenagers: 'I hope I can be as strong and as resilient as New York has been the past twenty years,' she said. 'Thank you for always having my back, thank you for cheering for me.' The relevant date – 9/11/01 – had been emblazoned just outside the tramlines on the court surface.

In the aftermath, as Raducanu sat on her courtside chair soaking it all in, the stadium sound system sparked up with 'Sweet Caroline', which the England football team had turned into the anthem of the English sporting summer. The small number of expats who had come along to support lustily led the singalong, and were joined by the player herself.

Each Grand Slam has a playbook about how it handles the singles champions in the immediate wake of winning their title. There is a largely pre-planned schedule of obligations to be fulfilled, with interviews to broadcast-rights-holders being a large part. Unbeknown to Raducanu, a series of outfits had been assembled beforehand for her to choose from, in which she could perform some of those duties. Much of the two hours which passed after the match involved her selecting a black dress and being made up. Then in the main press conference room she addressed the media. A nice touch introduced by the US Open is the champion presenting her coach with a trophy.

The self-effacing Richardson stepped forward from the wings. The winner was then whisked away to the main concourse in front of Arthur Ashe to show off her trophy to photographers, perched on the edge of the illuminated fountains. Often this ritual is performed away from the stadium at a city landmark, but with all the Covid restrictions it was considered more practical to keep it on-site this time.

Soon afterwards the tiny handful of British writers who had made it to New York were granted time with the new champion. The setting was modest as we sat around one of the dining tables in the media canteen, which had been mothballed in 2021 due to the small numbers of reporters in attendance. Given that face-to-face contact between players and writers had been so constrained, it was the first time I had properly sat down with her since the café in Sunderland eighteen months previously.

There was much to talk about, such as the congratulations she had just received from Her Majesty the Queen: 'I'm incredibly honoured, just blown away. I never in my life thought Her Majesty would watch one of my matches. It's so special, I can't believe that it's happening. I'm so grateful to have received that message,' she said.

It was a wide-ranging conversation, extending from the serious to reminders that here was someone only just into adulthood, who had done something truly extraordinary. The subject of the aspersions cast on her resolve after her Wimbledon exit was brought up, and she responded politely but firmly.

'At Wimbledon, I personally don't think it was a mental issue. The past week, I've shown a lot of mental resilience and toughness to face a lot of adversity. To go out on Ashe for the first time, I was nervous for sure. You could tell in the games where I went an early break down. Staying calm and staying in the moment has helped me through. You need a lot of mental strength to do it. I think that says something in itself.

'In the beginning, Arthur Ashe felt extremely big and I think I was a little bit thrown off. It took a bit of adjusting, but I absolutely love playing in front of that crowd. Even if it's not always for me, I just love hearing the noise. Today, it was extremely full – I didn't actually look up to the top very often, but when I did I just took it all in. I was very surprised by the number of people who wanted to watch me. It's crazy to think, three months ago I was in an exam hall and now I'm on the biggest court in the world.'

She also referenced her upbringing and the influence of her parents: 'The only pressure I was feeling was a pressure to perform. I think it's something I've always had, from a young age. It's been a part of my upbringing, thanks to my parents. It has helped throughout my whole life. Especially on Arthur Ashe Stadium, you need every ounce of help and experience that you can get. My mum is definitely a very strong person and I'm very inspired by her.'

Earlier that day, back in England prior to the final, the surreal nature of it all had been underlined by Renee quietly honouring a commitment she had made to the local tennis scene. She had turned up at Sundridge Park Tennis Club for a couple of hours, to pick up her daughter's Kent Player of the Year award.

This only added to the sense of general incredulity at what had happened. Nobody had taken the elevator from the basement to the sport's penthouse suite in such record time. The new champion had successfully managed to insulate herself from outside pressures, locking herself away in her New York hotel room at night listening to jazz, watching TV and ordering Uber Eats. Her new-found wealth was a source of amazement: 'Before my first-round qualifying match, I lost my AirPods three minutes before I was called to court. I was running around looking for them. I have been telling myself before each match, "If you win, you can buy yourself another pair of AirPods." That has been the running joke.'

Told that she had now reached more than a million followers on Instagram, she was so disbelieving that she needed to be shown a phone with her account on it: 'No! What?! It's changed to an M now, not a K! That's incredible. I can't believe it. I got an M! Wow. I had no idea. I just completely switched off from everything, gave my phone away. I haven't had a chance to catch up. I haven't checked my phone yet, I've got no idea what's going on.' According to research from the Women's Sport Trust, there were to be 8 million UK Google searches for Raducanu's name that month, as opposed to 250 in May.

In the same room we separately got to talk with Richardson, the Grand Slam-winning coach who had struggled to deliver on his own potential as a player. The softly spoken giant had set out to stay in the background as a quietly supportive presence throughout their extended stay in America that had begun back in San Francisco, and had concentrated on trying to block out the gathering hype and keep his player focused on the fundamentals.

'It's really been a case of having this mantra throughout the trip: just try and make the most of every day. We haven't got ahead of ourselves. We stayed in that zone of thinking short term and taking care of what's in front of her. And she's done that throughout the whole trip.'

Clearly the length of their relationship, going back to her formative tennis years in Bromley, had been a key factor: 'I've known Emma a long time. I think she has many strengths and some of them you can see, some you can't. For me, the biggest strength is the mind. Everything starts with the mind. And I think that strength has shown throughout this trip, not just here in the US Open. In Chicago and in Landisville she went through some very tough situations and matches and conditions. She managed to get through those situations, had the resilience and the toughness. She showed that not just here in New York, but the weeks before – her ability to deal with adversity and compete.

'She started to gain confidence from Chicago. You then gain momentum. Players start seeing the results and start viewing you differently. I go back to qualifying [in New York] and she beat some good players. In the second round she was down in the second set. People have to remember that she played ten matches in New York, but she came into qualifying having played five matches in tough conditions in Chicago. Five matches in Landisville. The mental strength that she has is truly special. She's been in this bubble, almost, with the team. So that's been really helpful for her. She's been able to focus on tennis and not get caught up in some of the things back home, but her life has changed now.'

It was well past 10 p.m. before all her obligations were finally done, and the tournament would lay on transport back to Manhattan. The team and some of those who had contributed to the fortnight jumped into a van and they rumbled down the Expressway for the last time to an appropriate soundtrack.

'After Emma had done all her commitments and photos we all climbed into a minibus,' recounted Tim Henman. 'Someone put on "Sweet Caroline" and I've got this great video on my phone of everyone singing along to it.'

The Presidential Suite had been booked, and instead of venturing out into what was left of the night the small group tucked into champagne and a sushi feast, looking back on the astonishing events of recent weeks: 'It was a very special night, and a real privilege to be invited and be there,' said Henman. 'We reminisced and talked about everything that has happened in the past few weeks. It was such a happy occasion and everyone really enjoyed themselves.' At 4.45 a.m. he retired for the night, but the new champion was still going strong, adrenaline and excitement still coursing through her.

While she celebrated on, some of us were getting up, ready for a long stint at the keyboard. There was, it has to be admitted, a hint of mixed emotion for the long-time observer. The whole week had been among the greatest things we could have been lucky enough to witness, something truly uplifting. This was coupled with a slight frisson of anxiety, given the history of those who have achieved great things in women's tennis at a tender age. At the end of my sixth piece filed that Sunday for the *Daily Mail* was an attempt to distil the sense of the immediate past and the future: 'Her values will be tested at times in the coming years – tennis does that to young people. But that can wait. Better now to reflect on two weeks that were spontaneous, innocent and utterly glorious.'

A proud father is reunited with his daughter as the new US Open champion arrives back in Bromley.

9

TENNIS COMES HOME

Nobody had taken much notice when Emma Raducanu slipped out of the UK on 24 July 2021, en route to San Francisco with her kitbags and Andrew Richardson for company. Naturally it was very different when she finally arrived home on 16 September. After flying into Heathrow overnight on the Thursday, she was ushered through to a pair of waiting black Range Rovers, replete with a security detail, and then spirited back to her cul-de-sac in Bromley for the reunion with her parents. Awaiting was also a large reception party of photographers, and after unloading her luggage she dutifully posed for pictures on the front lawn, with her father joining her, somewhat reluctantly.

By now she had already received her first taste of how life had changed since slamming down the winning ace, five days previously, that had clinched the title. Tennis players rarely hang around long after their business at a tournament is done, especially when home is the next destination. Nights spent in one's own bed are too precious for that. She, however, had been in no mood to rush back and she really meant it when she said she wanted to take in some of New York, having been locked into the hotel-to-tennis routine for three weeks.

The intimate party following the victory had gone on through the night and, despite dawn coming up soon after they got to bed, Richardson and Henman were still buzzing. After a couple of hours' sleep the two old friends were back in contact with each other and agreed to meet up for coffee before going for a long walk around Central Park together. There was still so much to reflect upon before they prepared to take their flights home on Monday evening. That was after the men's final on Sunday, which would see another new champion crowned in Russia's Daniil Medvedev, who was to deny Novak Djokovic the holy grail of a calendar Grand Slam.

Raducanu was more in recovery mode ahead of what would be an extremely long and busy Monday. Back in the UK, that morning's newspapers were united in devoting acres of print to her achievement and she adorned all their covers. In fact, the supremely photogenic recent A-level student was now being accorded the same status as the country's highest-profile individuals, and it would stay that way. For instance, from early July to the end of November 2021 a picture of her would be used on the front page of the *Daily Telegraph* no fewer than fifteen times. This is the very rarefied territory of someone like Boris Johnson, or the top royals such as the Duke and Duchess of Cambridge.

With requests coming in from around the world, it was decided she would be doing the rounds of America's coast-to-coast breakfast TV shows, *Today* and *Good Morning America*, at their Midtown studios just a short hop from her hotel. She charmed her purring hosts, telling *Good Morning America*, 'I'm trying to let this moment sink in. I had a really nice night with my team on the night of the final and we just discussed and reflected upon our incredible three weeks.'

The story of the missing AirPods, originally lost in the locker room, was a topic of some fascination, in light of her £1.8 million pay cheque. 'It's funny because actually the day before my semi-final, they found them – two and a half weeks later. It was like a great omen and I knew it was going to be a great day,' she said.

Then there was the long preparation for her evening's booking, the Met Gala at the Metropolitan Museum of Art, a charity fundraiser that attracts an A-list crowd of celebrities. Its proximity to the US Open makes it a regular fixture for top tennis players and the invitation came from one of the sport's superfans, *Vogue* supremo Anna Wintour. Raducanu found herself placed in the hands of styling professionals as she prepared to be seated on the Chanel table. She wore one of the famous design house's dazzling outfits, matched with jewellery from Tiffany's worth more than £30,000.

Tickets for the event could cost as much as £20,000 – it was a somewhat different affair to the university freshers' week parties that her friends from Newstead Wood would have been attending at around the same time.

While the likes of her final opponent Leylah Fernandez and former champion Naomi Osaka were there, the guest list also included British actresses such as Emily Blunt and Sienna Miller. As an avid motorsport fan, the attendee she most wanted to talk to was another guest, Lewis Hamilton.

'We had a really good conversation there,' she later reported. 'He's just been really cool and helping me. He said, "Be patient. You've just got to ride the wave." He's been such a good role model for me, and in terms of helping me out and through these next stages.'

The next day it was time to tick something else off the bucket list – a visit to the trading floor on Wall Street. This was, according to those close to her, the thing she had insisted on doing above all. Before that there was a congratulatory phone call from Boris Johnson. Downing Street issued a somewhat stiff summary of what they had talked about, couched in the language of some diplomatic meeting: 'Both the Prime Minister and Emma agreed on the importance of continuing to support grassroots tennis, and in encouraging young people to take up the game,' it read.

Down at Wall Street she was clapped onto the floor of the New York Stock Exchange. Onlookers were struck by just how genuinely curious she was about its workings, stopping to look at screens and asking traders how they operated. Wilfred Frost, British presenter of CNBC's *Closing Bell* programme, asked if she would do an impromptu interview for his show and she was happy to oblige, explaining why she was so fascinated by that world. 'It is something I have been studying at school, in my A-levels. I just always had a keen interest. My parents were both in finance and to see it live is incredible,' she told him.

Finally, on Wednesday night, it was time to go home. Anyone buying stock in Raducanu would have seen it skyrocket over the course of the summer, measured in the meritocracy of the tennis rankings. She had first stepped onto the grass courts as the world No. 366, and now she was leaving New York at No. 23.

In London the Lawn Tennis Association was seeking to ride the wave as well, in the never-ending pursuit of trying to get more people to take up the game. Electronic billboards around the capital were emblazoned with pictures of the four British winners in New York (Joe Salisbury, Alfie Hewett and Gordon Reid as well), declaring that 'Tennis Came Home'. An official homecoming event at Roehampton, hosted by the BBC's Clare Balding, was hastily arranged for the following week.

Back in Bromley there were decisions to be made about her tournament schedule. When it came to plotting when and where to play for the rest of the season, the options were limited. The BNP Paribas Open in Indian Wells in southern California was looming at the start of October, postponed from its usual March slot, but with the Asian swing of events entirely cancelled due to continuing Covid issues, the choices were distinctly narrowed after that. Complicating the equation was that Raducanu was now in fourteenth place to qualify for the eight-player year-end finals in Mexico, something unthinkable four weeks previously.

The coaching position also required immediate attention. The fact was that the spectacularly successful arrangement with Richardson had been made as a short-term one, and it had officially come to an end once that last ace had been slammed down at Flushing Meadows. On the logic that 'if it ain't broke don't fix it', renewing the deal seemed a no-brainer. Not only had the partnership with the genial giant yielded remarkable results, but his retention would also provide a measure of stability at a time when her world had been turned upside down. Not extending would certainly add to all the white noise.

The Raducanus had never gone with the flow on the coaching front, however, Emma being an advocate of personal resourcefulness and Ian a strong believer in a particular person being required for specific circumstances, even specific shots. Now that she had been catapulted to the highest echelons of the WTA Tour, Richardson's lack of long-term experience of that environment, and the players found there, counted against him.

When she turned up at Roehampton for the set-piece homecoming, broadcast on the BBC, it was inevitable she would be asked what her coaching plans were. A few jaws dropped to the floor when she revealed that, after talks, these would not involve the man who had guided her across North America.

'After Wimbledon, I was ranked around 200 in the world and at the time I thought Andrew would be a great coach to trial, so we went to the States,' she said. 'But never did I even dream of winning the US Open and having the run I did, and now I'm ranked 22 in the world, which is pretty crazy to me [her ranking had gone up another place by then]. I feel like at this stage in my career, and playing the top players in the world, I really need someone that has had that WTA Tour experience at the high levels, which means that I'm looking for someone who has been at that level and knows what it takes.'

Richardson, who would have been prepared to continue on adjusted terms, probably understood how Nigel Sears may have felt after Wimbledon. The parting had not been easy: 'Obviously, having such an experience with your team, it's tough to have that conversation with anyone,' she admitted.

While providing a first brush with controversy, the underlying truth of the matter is that coaches change regularly, especially in women's tennis and even more so in the period towards the end of the season. It is a time for reassessment, and the women have a longer off-season than their male counterparts. Nonetheless, it was sad that the undeserving Richardson had become another statistic of that reality. Soon a cluster of the bigger names were being linked with her, although with a self-starter like the new US Open champion it was possible to overstate the significance of the whole subject of coaching.

More positively, the following week saw British tennis gain what might be termed its first Raducanu dividend. The government announced it would contribute £22 million of taxpayer money towards a much-needed drive to renovate public courts throughout Britain (the LTA would add a further £8.5 million). There was clearly some capital in hitching the wagons to the young star.

No permanent new coach would be in place by the time she accepted a wild card for **Indian Wells** and jetted off there. On temporary coaching duty was her existing LTA 'case manager', Jeremy Bates, who was working at the tournament primarily with his established charge, Katie Boulter. Raymond Sarmiento, who had hit with her in San Francisco after Wimbledon, was also brought in for the week.

She was soon getting a taste of her new celebrity, with crowds packing out their practice sessions in the California desert sun, and security shadowing her every move. She was going to try and make the best of it: 'At the end of the day you're out there on your own and you have to be your own coach on the court, so I'm pretty comfortable,' she said before her return to action.

It was all somewhat unfamiliar, and not just because Richardson was absent and also (temporarily) Will Herbert. The courts at Indian Wells were described by Andy Murray as 'ridiculously slow', very different to New York. Raducanu was now a target and the first player taking aim was world No. 100 Aliaksandra Sasnovich, who had formerly been in the top thirty. Not only that, the Belarusian had already won a round because her opponent had received a bye through to their meeting in the second.

Sasnovich duly played up and Raducanu played down, with a notable absence of the positive intent and body language seen in New York. The result was a 6–2, 6–4 defeat. 'I think that what happened tonight was just down to experience,' she reasoned. 'I've got a very long future ahead of me, potentially fifteen, twenty years in the game. My priority is that longevity, and I'm at the very start. So I just need to cut myself slack. I'm in a good place mentally. I'm looking at it in big-picture terms. This is going to be very small in the long term.'

This visit to the United States was not remotely the same happy experience as the previous one. Strangely, though, there was a parallel to New York in that the prestigious tournament threw up a surprise British winner in one of the singles events. We went for Emma Raducanu, we got Cam Norrie, who beat Nikoloz Basilashvili of Georgia in the final.

Raducanu's early defeat banished the possibility of qualifying for the year-end finals, which had been relocated to Mexico from China. One option would have been to close down the season there and then. So quick had been her progress that there were obvious gaps that required some filling in, one being the hard grind of building up the necessary reserves of fitness and strength. Most of her peers had been undergoing this process for years, rather than sitting in exam halls, and it is not something that can be achieved overnight. Yet shutting down 2021 would have sent out a negative signal, and there was another line of thinking, too: that it was better to gain more precious exposure to the tour and get some of the post-US Open hype out of the way, bringing forward the likely reality check.

*   *   *

Hype comes in many different shapes and forms, and in the wake of Flushing Meadows there was feverish speculation about Raducanu's potential earnings from endorsements. Given her talent, looks, intelligence and add-ons like the ability to speak Chinese, there was much for marketing experts to salivate over when it came to estimating what she might make off the court. Numbers were plucked out of the air, and it was clear that Nike and Wilson would not remain her only sponsors. Soon Tiffany and Dior were on board, although the former had been in the pipeline before she won the US title.

A by-product was that when the inevitable losses came, a connection would be made automatically between the on-court setbacks and attending galas or promoting a product. What was unexpected was the source that would turbocharge the speculation in this area. England rugby coach Eddie Jones was not known for any particular interest in tennis, but he chose to make Raducanu a reference when talking to the rugby media during the 2021 autumn internationals. The point he was attempting to make, in light of all the noise around his emerging star fly-half Marcus Smith, was that there can be competing interests for those who gain a high profile through their sporting deeds.

'The big thing for good young players is distractions,' said Jones. 'There's a reason why the young girl who won the US Open hasn't done so well afterwards. What have you seen her on – the front page of *Vogue* and *Harper's Bazaar* or whatever it is, wearing Christian Dior clothes.'

In terms of clumsiness he achieved pretty much the full house with those two sentences – inaccuracy, poor choice of language, unfairness. At the time, Raducanu had lost only two matches and won two since the US Open. The *Vogue* shoot had actually been done around Wimbledon, not New York. At Indian Wells, Jeremy Bates had talked of her continued desire to be 'on it' every day. After a swift backlash, slightly reminiscent of the furore surrounding John McEnroe's Wimbledon comments, Jones wrote a letter explaining his comments and apologising for any offence caused. The player herself laughed it away when asked to respond, and claimed – probably disingenuously – that she did not know what had been said. Notably, in her press conferences she began emphasising that nothing would be getting in the way of the hard grind of training.

It was an early lesson, however, in how perceptions change when you are breathing the rarefied air of being one of the best-known people in the whole country. Certainly an appearance at London's Royal Albert Hall in late September to walk the red carpet at the premiere of the new James Bond film had only added to her profile. Harmless in itself, it had come fairly swiftly after the Met Gala evening – and people are apt to put two and two together in these circumstances to make different numbers.

Ironically, there had been nothing starry at all about her second tournament after the US Open, nor the means of transport used to get there. After Indian Wells, it was decided to play two more official events on the WTA Tour, relatively small ones at the level offering $250,000 prize money. The first of these was the **Transylvania Open** in Cluj-Napoca in Romania, which would bring with it the dimension of her returning to the country of her father's birth. An immediate subject of fascination was whether her beloved grandmother, Niculina, would attend. Several times Raducanu had spoken fondly of the numerous trips to visit her in Bucharest, and how she loved her home cooking of traditional dishes such as sarmale, a concoction of pork and cabbage leaves.

Yet where the tournament is situated, in the north of the country, is not easily accessible, either from the Romanian capital or from London. The only direct UK flight was from Luton with budget airline Wizz Air, and so it was that Raducanu – accompanied by father Ian – joined the hordes at Britain's least fashionable airport for the three-hour journey. One concession to her new-found fame was being ushered through the VIP lanes straight towards the plane. It was also badly delayed, meaning she arrived late into the night. As for a visit while she was in Cluj from her eighty-eight-year-old grandmother, that proved impossible. The reasons were not just the eight-hour journey, but also a fast-developing Covid wave and impending semi-lockdown in the country, where cases were spiralling.

Cluj turned out to be an unexpected delight for the posse of reporters from the UK who travelled – at least until a 9 p.m. curfew was imposed on the Monday in response to the gathering crisis. As a city full of baroque architecture and spectacular churches, with associations with Bram Stoker's *Dracula*, it was easy to see why it is considered one of Europe's less exploited gems. Sadly for the tournament and its hospitable organisers, spectators at sports events were banned by the government from the Monday when the main draw began. With the country's tennis fans having taken some ownership of Raducanu – a common surname in Romania – there were thousands who wanted to see her.

In the event, they could only watch her public practice sessions over the preceding weekend. Both of these were against Elena-Gabriela Ruse, one of the Romanian WTA stars with whom she had become friendly. The talk was soon of how the host nation's players had taken a shine to their British cousin who, it turned out, could make a decent fist of speaking her grandmother's language.

Ian Raducanu was also a subject of fascination for the local media, although he was turning down all requests from television crews. Still not having met him due to his usual absence from tournaments and the restrictions of the last two years, I sought out and approached the father of the UK's newest sports sensation in between practice sessions. Casually dressed, he had been discreetly watching from the shadows of the large and impressive BT Arena and was not easy to spot. After introducing myself, and the understanding being that he was not in the market for interviews, we had a pleasant conversation about tennis, coaching and the ways of the media. It was very cordial, if not especially revealing. But then as I walked away the realisation dawned on me, a slightly odd one for an experienced journalist used to finding out about people's backgrounds: he had asked me more questions than I had been able to ask him.

When the main draw began in Cluj it felt like a reversion to the dark days: no public allowed in and the sound of the ball and the umpire's calls echoing around the venue. The event's resident Dracula impersonator did his best to liven things up, but it had a melancholy feel. On the court Raducanu's first opponent was the experienced Slovenian Polona Hercog, best known for once having played a dramatic match against Coco Gauff on the Centre Court at Wimbledon. Hercog played as if her life depended on it, as did all three of the opponents that week – again a contrast to some of those ranged against Raducanu at Flushing Meadows. This time the US Open champion was much more assertive in coming back from a set down to see her off, and she followed it up by beating the host country's Ana Bogdan.

She then lost in the quarter-finals, 6–2, 6–1, to Marta Kostyuk, the nineteen-year-old from Ukraine who had been an early developer, making the third round of the Australian Open at just fifteen. Two things stood out. First, Raducanu had, before the match, talked up the fact that Kostyuk had comfortably beaten her in the juniors. The Ukrainian said afterwards that she took confidence hearing that, which may have been another lesson to learn. Secondly, the difference in their physical condition was clear. While the British player had often been at school, Kostyuk had trained like a pro since her early teens. Despite being only five months older, those years of work showed in her physique and the power she could call on. No wonder Raducanu was already talking of the pre-season training block's importance.

One more tournament remained, and this was to be the last – at least for a while – that would be played without a coach. With no direct flights to Linz for the **Upper Austria Ladies Open**, Raducanu would fly by private jet this time, for what turned out to be a short stay. She lost to another opponent playing well above her ranking, China's Wang Xinyu, and afterwards confirmed that the search for a coach was over.

In the way of the modern world's social media, it turned out that a picture had emerged from September, via a fan account on Instagram, of her meeting with Torben Beltz in a Bromley coffee shop, which was duly reported by the *Telegraph*. The German, a former journeyman player, was in the process of splitting from Angelique Kerber, the three-time Grand Slam champion. Kerber had served a long apprenticeship on the tour before breaking through, following a similar trajectory to someone like Simona Halep. Beltz had helped his compatriot to win Wimbledon and the Australian and US Opens, and was known as an accommodating coach rather than a my-way-or-the-highway sort of operator. Now he would be the latest in the long line of those developing Raducanu.

He had not been one of the higher-profile names associated with the job, but his work in transforming Kerber had been noted: 'I think that experience definitely helps with someone as inexperienced as me,' she commented while in Romania. 'He can help guide me through, which I feel really confident about. Also, he's a really positive, cheerful guy who brings great energy to the team.'

Before the off-season hard work began there was a week's holiday in the Caribbean, where Raducanu could indulge her passion for speed in learning to jet-ski. Then it was back to the grind of several weeks' physical training, interrupted only by an exhibition back at the Royal Albert Hall, now transformed into a tennis venue and not the site of a film premiere. As a child she had been taken there by her father to watch the long-established

Seniors' event, now run by her management company, IMG. He had taken her to watch the veteran singles players, but she had been more interested in the tricks of French-Iranian showman Mansour Bahrami, who had been pleasing crowds for years.

For her first match on home soil since Wimbledon or the US Open she chose Elena-Gabriela Ruse as her opponent. The match was largely meaningless, a glorified practice session in which ballkids were occasionally handed rackets to play with. What the reception she received at the historic venue confirmed, along with the speed of ticket sales, was her popularity among the public.

Within days Jo Konta, the British No. 1 she had replaced, announced her retirement. Konta had made late withdrawals from both Wimbledon and the US Open, the former due to Covid, the latter due to problems with her knees and thighs. Hers had been a distinguished career, but one over which the shadows had fallen with unlikely speed, partly because of the rise of Raducanu. This constituted a remarkable bit of dovetailing – British tennis was immensely fortunate that as one totemic player left, another one had arrived.

With coach Torben Beltz in Melbourne during the 2022 Australian Open.

10

LEARNINGS

The festive period of late 2020 had seen Emma Raducanu combine playing a couple of low-key domestic tournaments before Christmas with her continuing A-level studies.

Twelve months on it was all rather different, surreally so. While her contemporaries from school were coming home for the holidays from university, she was holed up at a resort hotel in Abu Dhabi, in enforced isolation after contracting Covid. There was another small detail. While serving her time in solitary confinement she would be presented, remotely, with the BBC Sports Personality of the Year award, following three-times winner Andy Murray as the latest representative from tennis.

Aside from anything, it was another example of how dramatically her life had diverged from those of her schoolmates. A month later, now in Australia, she reflected on how things had changed, and how it made keeping in touch with old friends difficult at times. 'There are moments when I'm not on my phone replying to people and I feel guilty,' she told British reporters in Melbourne. 'But I'm prioritising my work, and we're very fortunate with what we get to do and the places we get to go in travelling the world.'

Raducanu, setting out for her first full year on the tour, had been learning that the best-laid schemes can be wrecked by circumstances, especially in the time of Covid. The idea had been to play in the grandiosely named Mubadala World Tennis Championship exhibition event in Abu Dhabi before Christmas, as part of a specifically programmed off-season building towards the Australian Open. The Omicron variant, however, had other plans. On 13 December she announced that she was having to withdraw after returning a positive test. She would not be alone, as the virus ran rampant through the locker rooms there and the majority of participants, including Rafael Nadal, would also be afflicted.

Isolation is a grim experience, although her newly elevated status would ensure that hers would be more comfortable than others. She was in a suite at the luxury Rixos Premium Saadiyat Island hotel, with its own outside space to stretch out in as she whiled away the time getting rid of the virus, which gave her only mild symptoms. As she reported later, she would sleep in until lunchtime, watch some motor sport and keep herself active by concentrating on racking up 10,000 steps a day by walking around.

Breaking up the drudgery was the evening of 19 December when, seated in front of closed curtains, she accepted a replica of the award which had been delivered to her. 'To win, it's pretty amazing. I've watched *Sports Personality of the Year* growing up, so I'm really humbled to join the amazing past winners', she said.

Unlike so much of what had happened in 2021, it could hardly have been called a surprise, even though no woman had won the award in fifteen years (Zara Phillips had been the last one). Finishing ahead of diver Tom Daley and swimmer Adam Peaty, she had been the strong favourite and became the first female tennis player to receive the accolade since Virginia Wade in 1977.

By now Andrew Richardson, the coach who had accompanied her on the great adventure in America which had led to all this, was far away from the scene. No seeker of the limelight, he had melted away from sight since their split in late September. Richardson had decided to have time out and take stock after what had happened, devoting attention to his two tennis-playing young sons. They spent a few autumn weeks at the academy belonging to former world No. 1 Juan Carlos Ferrero in Alicante, Spain. At the time of the *SPOTY* presentation he was actually at a tournament in America with his son Rocco – the junior Orange Bowl in Florida, where Raducanu had once played.

While the BBC award was gratifying, it was clear that the untimely Covid diagnosis would wreak havoc with the plans to build up the new US Open champion physically for the coming season. With isolation complete, and having flown on to Australia from Dubai, there was much catching-up to do. Too much, it was decided, for her to play in her first scheduled tournament of the season. The new year dawned with her pulling out of the initial WTA event in Melbourne to try and get some more time on the practice court. Happier news was the confirmation – it had been heavily trailed by government sources – that she was receiving an MBE in the latest Honours List.

The extent to which she was short of a gallop became clear when she travelled to **Sydney** to play in the week before the **Australian Open**. Her opponent was the world No. 13 Elena Rybakina and it felt like another of those 'Welcome to the tour' moments. Their first-round match was all over in fifty-five minutes and a 6–0, 6–1 defeat. The loss was not unexpected, although the scale of it came as a shock. Afterwards Raducanu and Torben Beltz, her new coach, found an adjacent court in an attempt to iron out some wrinkles. She explained later that, in terms of preparation, there had been some anxiety about going too hard after her period of inactivity.

'I didn't go into full training, because that's probably the easiest way to get injured,' she said. 'It's just me being a step slow, a step behind. She was sharper and more match-tight than I was. After the match I got a box of balls and went straight to the practice court. I felt like I could have done some things better in the match, and I wanted to try and fix it straight away, just leave with a better feeling about it.'

Her appearance at the first Grand Slam since New York attracted less attention than might have been the case. In that week, the tennis world was still convulsed by the drama surrounding

Novak Djokovic and his attempts to play the tournament despite being unvaccinated. By the time Raducanu was giving her pre-tournament press conference on the Saturday, the extraordinary situation was continuing to unfold, the nine-time champion being back in an immigration detention hotel while a second court hearing took place about his presence in Australia.

The whole saga could be seen as one of the four enormous stories that the sport had provided over an eight-month period. They had all reached an audience far beyond the sport's normal constituency: Naomi Osaka going on media-duties strike at the French Open; a qualifier winning the US Open; the disappearance of Chinese player Peng Shuai; and now the Djokovic episode in Melbourne. The sport of tennis can rumble along fairly anonymously at times, but when it goes big it goes nuclear.

Events elsewhere meant that Raducanu drawing Sloane Stephens, another US Open champion, was not headline news. The other 255 players originally entered into the singles draws not called Djokovic regretted the fact that the usual tournament matters were being overlooked. Asked her view, Raducanu said, 'I feel it has taken away a little bit from the great tennis that's been happening over this summer in Australia. For example, Andy Murray, he's in the final tonight [at the Sydney Classic], which I think is pretty incredible.' Regarding her wider prospects ahead of the Stephens match, she was trying to look at it in the round: 'Twelve months ago I was just in my room studying for my exams, I was watching from afar [the 2021 edition had actually taken place in February]. I just feel very grateful to have this opportunity to play here. I think that's one thing, I need to just relax. As long as the trend is trending upwards, just a matter of small fluctuations, I think I can be proud.'

This sentiment was echoed in a roundabout way in a TV commercial released by Nike to coincide with the Open. Lasting less than twenty seconds, it reflected on the various commentary around her (which by and large had remained sympathetic). It showed her hitting on a court with large words flashing up on a backdrop: distracted, perfect, fluke, flawless, one-hit wonder. In time probably none of those things would prove to be true, and certainly not all at once. Having announced additional sponsorship deals with Evian and British Airways in December, however, it was sure that her endorsements would continue to be a subject of scrutiny.

Beating Stephens would not be conclusive in knocking down the 'one-hit wonder' assertion, but it was a good start. The American had shown many times that, on her day, she was a match for anyone, but her form was uncertain, given that she had not played recently and had got married at the start of the month. What transpired was a fascinating contest which took Raducanu into new territory – a deciding set at a Grand Slam. She responded admirably in a match whose surges were slightly reminiscent of what had been witnessed in New York. The second round was reached with the undulating scoreline of 6–0, 2–6, 6–1.

The more noteworthy post-match comments came from Stephens, who brought something of an edge to her assessment of their encounter. 'I was talking to someone in the locker room and I'm like, "We'll be here when she comes down,"' she said, before slightly checking herself. 'Not Emma, but just in general. It all is like a cycle, and I think learning how to deal with it early on is the best way to handle it. Just because there's always a lot of ups and downs in tennis. Because she is so young it's definitely a long road, so there's going to be a lot of ups and downs. I think she has just a lot to learn.'

For all the vaguely acerbic talk, it was an encouraging result for Raducanu, but forty-eight hours later it became clear that there would be a price to pay for the missed hours on court around Christmas and the New Year. This came in the shape of a nasty blister on the racket hand which would hamper her, and force her into creativity, in her second-round match against Danka Kovinić of Montenegro. Necessity is the mother of invention and she was obliged to play a lot of swished, undercut forehands to take the pressure off her hand. The makeshift groundstroke failed to gain her the win, although it was close, as she lost 6–3 in another third set. Some players can be put off by a discomfited opponent, but Kovinić stuck stoically to her task.

Afterwards Raducanu revealed that one opinion among her team had been that she should withdraw altogether, but she had chosen to give it a try: 'I was proud of how I kept fighting even in those situations where I was "I'm really struggling here, I can't really do much," but I just kept hanging in there.

'I have been struggling with blisters since I started playing really in Australia, because twenty-one days, no tennis, my hands got pretty soft. From day one, day two, I was getting blisters pop up here and there. This particular one has been with me for about five days. I have been trying to tape it for every practice, and it would harden and dry out, but then once I would play again, another layer would just keep ripping off.

'Because I'm still young, I feel like I can learn a backhand, I can learn some sort of tactics, but it's quite hard to learn that fight and grittiness to hang in there when things are pretty much all against you.'

She was out of the tournament by the first Thursday night, and this is the lot of most tennis players. There are 256 who start out in the singles of a Grand Slam on a Monday, and four days later 192 of them have lost and are gone. She had been denied a third-round match against one of her childhood idols, Simona Halep.

Raducanu stayed on for the weekend before heading back home, via a week-long stop in Singapore, to face up to the rest of a year bursting with possibilities. Before leaving Australia she gave a final reflection to reporters from the UK: 'It's definitely a lot of work to stay at the top. When I was lower down the ranks I thought that once you were in that top bracket you could stay there, but you can't. You pretty much have to be on it every week, be really focused and really work hard.'

Beyond all the hype and froth, that ability to relentlessly apply oneself, constantly adding to your armoury and defences, is the determining factor in sustaining success. It always is in an individual sport of global dimensions, one that gleams on the surface but ultimately rewards those who are prepared to grind away beneath its shiny exterior. As at the US Open, the thin margins in women's tennis were there for all to see in Melbourne, where the seeds were once again scattered. Only three of the top twenty were to make it through to the last eight.

For this particular nineteen-year-old there could be no surer attribute to help her than the quest for self-improvement. It had taken her a very long way from Bromley, to unforeseen heights via outposts such as Liverpool and Lisbon, Sunderland and Solapur. Whatever else happened, and wherever else this life took her, she would always have New York.

CAREER STATISTICS |

JUNIOR SINGLES RESULTS

2015

NIKE JUNIOR INTERNATIONAL, LIVERPOOL

16 November to 21 November 2015   Liverpool, Great Britain
Grade 5   Surface: Hard (indoor)
Main Draw   Entry: Wild Card

Final	W	v Lauryn John-Baptiste (GB)	6–1, 6–4
Semi-final	W	v Sophia Derivan (Ireland)	6–1, 6–2
Quarter-final	W	v Martina Paladini Jennings (GB)	6–2, 6–3
2nd Round	W	v Amarni Banks (GB)	6–2, 5–7, 6–4
1st Round	W	v Louie McLelland (GB)	6–4, 7–5

2016

NIKE JUNIOR INTERNATIONAL, BOURNEMOUTH

12 July to 16 July 2016   Bournemouth, Great Britain
Grade 4   Surface: Clay
Main Draw   Entry: Direct Acceptance

Final	L	v Hannah Mccolgan (GB)	7–6^5, 4–6, 2–6
Semi-final	W	v Marie Mattel (France)	6–4, 6–3
Quarter-final	W	v Maria Budin (GB)	7–6^7, 6–2
2nd Round	W	v Hannah Viller Møller (Denmark)	2–6, 6–2, 6–1
1st Round	W	v M J Changwereza (GB)	6–2, 6–2

LUXEMBOURG OUTDOOR JUNIOR OPEN 2016

1 August to 6 August 2016		Schifflange, Luxembourg	
Grade 4		Surface: Clay	
Main Draw		Entry: Direct Acceptance	
Final	L	v Eva Marie Voracek (Germany)	6–4, 4–6 ,6–7[3]
Semi-final	W	v Margaux Orange (France)	7–5, 6–4
Quarter-final	W	v Eva Vedder (Netherlands)	6–2, 6–3
2nd Round	W	v Mathilde Trigaux (Belgium)	6–2, 6–1
1st Round	W	v Merima Mujasevic (Luxembourg)	6–2, 6–1

VIERUMAKI JUNIOR CUP

26 October to 30 October 2016		Vierumaki, Finland	
Grade 4		Surface: Hard (indoor)	
Main Draw		Entry: Direct Acceptance	
Quarter-final	L	v Maria Lota Kaul (Estonia)	6–4, 4–6, 1–6
2nd Round	W	v Kristina Savvi (Russia)	6–3, 6–2
1st Round	W	v Frida Furst (Sweden)	6–4, 6–3

2017

YONEX ITF, HAMBURG

7 February to 12 February 2017		Hamburg, Germany	
Grade 4		Surface: Hard (indoor)	
Main Draw		Entry: Direct Acceptance	
Final	W	v Anastazja Rosnowska (Germany)	6–4, 6–2
Semi-final	W	v Denise-Antonela Stoica (Romania)	7–5, 6–3
Quarter-final	W	v Benedetta Ivaldi (Italy)	7–6[3], 6–2
3rd Round	W	v Lara Schmidt (Germany)	6–4, 6–1
2nd Round	W	v Reka Zadori (Hungary)	6–0, 7–5
1st Round	W	v Clarisse Bennoit (France)	6–1, 6–3

COPENHAGEN WINTER CUP

13 February to 18 February 2017   Copenhagen, Denmark
Grade 4   Surface: Hard (indoor)
Main Draw   Entry: Direct Acceptance
1st Round   L   v Clara Tauson (Denmark)   6–2, 3–6, 1–6

ITF OSLO OPEN

20 February to 25 February 2017   Oslo, Norway
Grade 4   Surface: Hard (indoor)
Main Draw   Entry: Direct Acceptance
Final   W   v Denise-Antonela Stoica (Romania)   6–1, 6–1
Semi-final   W   v Sopiko Tsitskishvili (Georgia)   6–0, 6–2
Quarter-final   W   v Melis Yasar (Sweden)   7–6^0, 6–0
2nd Round   W   v Sarina Reinertsen (Norway)   6–0, 6–1
1st Round   W   v Ida Ferding (Sweden)   6–1, 6–1

IV ITF JUNIOR GRIP2 TENNIS ACADEMY VINARÒS

21 March to 25 March 2017   Vinaròs, Spain
Grade 2   Surface: Clay
Main Draw   Entry: Qualifier
1st Round   L   v Eva Guerrero Álvarez (Spain)   2–6, 4–6
Qualifying Draw   Entry: Direct Acceptance
Quarter-final   W   v Laura López Giese (Spain)   6–4, 6–1
2nd Round   W   v Leyre Romero Gormaz (Spain)   7–6^5, 6–2
1st Round   W   v Carlota Martinez Cirez (Spain)   6–3, 6–2

XI ITF JUNIOR GRIP2 TENIS ACADEMY BENICARLÓ

28 March to 1 April 2017   Benicarló, Spain
Grade 2   Surface: Clay
Qualifying Draw   Entry: Direct Acceptance
2nd Round   L   v Lucía Marzal Martínez (Spain)   6–3, 2–6, 6–7^6
1st Round   W   v Laura López Giese (Spain)   6–1, 6–0

42ND CITY OF FLORENCE

11 April to 17 April 2017			Florence, Italy
Grade 2			Surface: Clay
Main Draw			Entry: Direct Acceptance
Quarter-final	L	v Barbora Matusova (Slovakia)	6–2, 5–7, 4–6
2nd Round	W	v Costanza Traversi (Italy)	6–0, 6–1
1st Round	W	v Veronika Erjavec (Slovenia)	7–5, 6–0

41ST MEDIAS-SEN-SIBIU JUNIOR ITF TOURNAMENT

25 April to 30 April 2017			Mediaş, Romania
Grade 2			Surface: Clay
Main Draw			Entry: Direct Acceptance
Quarter-final	L	v Georgia Andreea Crăciun (Romania)	3–6, 6–7[1]
2nd Round	W	v Andreea Prisăcariu (Romania)	6–4, 6–1
1st Round	W	v Fatima Keita (Romania)	6–0, 6–2

HODMEZOVASARHELY CUP

23 May to 27 May 2017			Hodmezovasarhely, Hungary
Grade 2			Surface: Clay
Main Draw			Entry: Direct Acceptance
1st Round	L	v Andreea Velcea (Romania)	4–6, 2–6

53RD ASTRID BOWL CHARLEROI, BELGIAN INTERNATIONAL JUNIOR CHAMPIONSHIPS

29 May to 3 June 2017			Charleroi-Marcinelle, Belgium
Grade 1			Surface: Clay
Main Draw			Entry: Qualifier
2nd Round	L	v Anhzelika Isaeva (Russia)	4–6, 6–7[4]
1st Round	W	v Katya Townsend (USA)	6–4, 6–3
Qualifying Draw			Entry: Direct Acceptance
3rd Round	W	v Svenja Ochsner (Switzerland)	6–4, 6–4
2nd Round	W	v Camille Townsend (USA)	6–1, 6–1
1st Round	Bye		

NIKE JUNIOR INTERNATIONAL, ROEHAMPTON

2 July to 7 July 2017		Roehampton, Great Britain	
Grade 1		Surface: Grass	
Main Draw		Entry: Wild Card	
1st Round	L	v Barbora Matusova (Slovakia)	2–6, 2–6

THE JUNIOR CHAMPIONSHIPS, WIMBLEDON

8 July to 16 July 2017		Wimbledon, Great Britain	
Grade A		Surface: Grass	
Main Draw		Entry: Wild Card	
2nd Round	L	v En Shuo Liang (Taipei)	1–6, 6–4, 6–8
1st Round	W	v Anastasia Kharitonova (Russia)	6–1, 6–3

2018

CHANDIGARH ITF JUNIORS

1 January to 6 January 2018		Chandigarh, India	
Grade 3		Surface: Hard	
Main Draw		Entry: Direct Acceptance	
Final	W	v Diana Khodan (Ukraine)	6–4, 6–4
Semi-final	W	v Ziva Falkner (Slovenia)	6–3, 6–2
Quarter-final	W	v Akanksha A Bhan (India)	6–1, 6–3
2nd Round	W	v Isabelle Haverlag (Netherlands)	6–1, 6–3
1st Round	W	v Prinkle Singh (India)	6–3, 6–1

DELHI ITF JUNIORS

8 January to 13 January 2018		New Delhi, India	
Grade 2		Surface: Hard	
Main Draw		Entry: Direct Acceptance	
Final	W	v Selin Övünç (Turkey)	6–2, 6–3
Semi-final	W	v Mai Napatt Nirundorn (Thailand)	6–2, 6–1
Quarter-final	W	v Vaidehi Chaudhari (India)	6–2, 4–2 (retired)

| 2nd Round | W | v Diana Khodan (Ukraine) | 4–6, 6–3, 6–1 |
| 1st Round | W | v Muskan Gupta (India) | 6–1, 6–3 |

BIOTEHNOS CUP

5 February to 11 February 2018   Chişinău, Moldova
Grade 2   Surface: Hard (indoor)
Main Draw   Entry: Direct Acceptance

Final	W	v Stefania Rogozińska Dzik (Poland)	6–3, 6–0
Semi-final	W	v Polina Kudermetova (Russia)	6–2, 6–1
Quarter-final	W	v Evgeniya Burdina (Russia)	6–1, 6–3
2nd Round	W	v Tamara Malešević (Serbia)	2–6, 6–0, 6–4
1st Round	W	v Isabella Tcherkes Zade (Italy)	1–6, 6–2, 6–2

SIAULIAI OPEN 2018

20 February to 25 February 2018   Siauliai, Lithuania
Grade 2   Surface: Hard (indoor)
Main Draw   Entry: Direct Acceptance

Final	W	v Stefania Rogozińska Dzik (Poland)	6–0, 6–4
Semi-final	W	v Caijsa Wilda Hennemann (Sweden)	6–1, 6–4
Quarter-final	W	v Alice Tubello (France)	6–3, 6–4
2nd Round	W	v Julia Avdeeva (Russia)	6–3, 7–5
1st Round	W	v Iveta Daujotaitė (Lithuania)	6–3, 6–3

ROLAND GARROS JUNIOR FRENCH CHAMPIONSHIPS

3 June to 9 June 2018   Paris, France
Grade A   Surface: Clay
Main Draw   Entry: Direct Acceptance

| 2nd Round | L | v Clara Tauson (Denmark) | 2–6, 1–6 |
| 1st Round | W | v Maria Timofeeva (Russia) | 6–4, 6–3 |

THE JUNIOR CHAMPIONSHIPS, WIMBLEDON

7 July to 15 July 2018		Wimbledon, Great Britain	
Grade A		Surface: Grass	
Main Draw		Entry: Direct Acceptance	
Quarter-final	L	v Iga Świątek (Poland)	0–6, 1–6
3rd Round	W	v Joanna Garland (Taipei)	7–5, 6–4
2nd Round	W	v Leylah Fernandez (Canada)	6–2, 6–4
1st Round	W	v Gabriella Price (USA)	6–1, 6–4

US OPEN JUNIOR TENNIS CHAMPIONSHIPS

2 September to 9 September 2018		New York, USA	
Grade A		Surface: Hard	
Main Draw		Entry: Direct Acceptance	
Quarter-final	L	v Clara Burel (France)	2–6, 0–6
3rd Round	W	v Qinwen Zheng (China)	7–6⁶, 6–1
2nd Round	W	v Alexa Noel (USA)	6–0, 6–1
1st Round	W	v Margaryta Bilokin (Ukraine)	6–3, 6–1

2019

J1 TRARALGON

11 January to 16 January 2019		Traralgon, Australia	
Grade 1		Surface: Hard	
Main Draw		Entry: Direct Acceptance	
Semi-final	L	v Clara Tauson (Denmark)	3–6, 6–3, 1–6
Quarter-final	W	v Anastasia Tikhonova (Russia)	6–1, 6–1
3rd Round	W	v Viktoryia Kanapatskaya (Belarus)	6–0, 4–6, 6–2
2nd Round	W	v Natsumi Kawaguchi (Japan)	6–4, 6–4
1st Round	W	v Sijia Wei (China)	6–3, 6–3

AUSTRALIAN OPEN JUNIOR CHAMPIONSHIPS

19 January to 26 January 2019			Melbourne, Australia
Grade A			Surface: Hard
Main Draw			Entry: Direct Acceptance
1st Round	L	v Himari Sato (Japan)	2–6, 5–7

J1 ROEHAMPTON

30 June to 5 July 2019			Roehampton, Great Britain
Grade 1			Surface: Grass
Main Draw			Entry: Wild Card
3rd Round	L	v Natsumi Kawaguchi (Japan)	2–6, 1–3 (retired)
2nd Round	W	v Séléna Janicijevic (France)	6–3, 5–7, 6–0
1st Round	W	v Carlota Martínez Círez (Spain)	6–1, 7–5

THE JUNIOR CHAMPIONSHIPS, WIMBLEDON

6 July to 14 July 2019			Wimbledon, Great Britain
Grade A			Surface: Grass
Main Draw			Entry: Wild Card
1st Round	L	v Martyna Kubka (Poland)	6–0, 1–6, 5–7

WOMEN'S SINGLES RESULTS

2018

ITF $15,000, NANJING (1)

26 March to 1 April 2018		Nanjing, China	
ITF Women's Circuit		Surface: Hard	
Qualifying Draw		Entry: Direct Acceptance	
3rd Round	L	v Siqi Cao (China)	4–6, 2–6
2nd Round	W	v Oleksandra Oliynykova (Croatia)	7–6^2, 6–1
1st Round	W	v Satsuki Koike (Japan)	6–0, 6–0

ITF $15,000, NANJING (2)

2 April to 8 April 2018		Nanjing, China	
ITF Women's Circuit		Surface: Hard	
Main Draw		Entry: Qualifier	
Quarter-final	L	v Xiaodi You (China)	6–7^4 (retired)
2nd Round	W	v Sofia Smagina (Russia)	6–3, 6–4
1st Round	W	v Wushuang Zheng (China)	6–4, 6–4
Qualifying Draw		Entry: Direct Acceptance	
3rd Round	W	v Kwan Yau Ng (Hong Kong)	6–4, 6–1
2nd Round	W	v Ho Ching Wu (Hong Kong)	6–2, 6–1
1st Round	W	v Yunqi He (China)	6–0, 6–0

ITF $15,000, TIBERIAS

14 May to 20 May 2018		Tiberias, Israel	
ITF Women's Circuit		Surface: Hard	
Main Draw		Entry: Qualifier	
Final	W	v Hélène Scholsen (Belgium)	7–5, 6–4
Semi-final	W	v Vlada Ekshibarova (Israel)	6–3, 6–0
Quarter-final	W	v Laetitia Pulchartová (Czech Rep)	6–2, 6–1

2nd Round	W	v Melis Sezer (Turkey)	6–1, 6–4
1st Round	W	v Madison Bourguignon (USA)	6–4, 6–3
Qualifying Draw		Entry: Direct Acceptance	
2nd Round	W	v Jane Stewart (USA)	6–1, 6–2
1st Round	Bye		

ITF/TENNIS EUROPE $100,000, MANCHESTER

11 June to 17 June 2018	Manchester, Great Britain
ITF Women's Circuit	Surface: Grass
Main Draw	Entry: Wild Card

| 1st Round | L | v Harriet Dart (GB) | 3–6, 6–3, 1–6 |

THE CHAMPIONSHIPS, WIMBLEDON

2 July to 15 July 2018	Wimbledon, Great Britain
Grand Slam	Surface: Grass
Qualifying Draw	Entry: Wild Card

| 1st Round | L | v Barbora Stefkova (Czech Rep) | 4–6, 7–5, 2–6 |

ITF/TENNIS EUROPE $25,000, LISBON

17 September to 23 September 2018	Lisbon, Portugal
ITF Women's Circuit	Surface: Hard
Qualifying Draw	Entry: Direct Acceptance

| 2nd Round | L | v Shalimar Talbi (Belarus) | 6–7^4, 2–6 |
| 1st Round | W | v Miriam Medina Cardeña (Spain) | 6–0, 6–0 |

ITF/TENNIS EUROPE $15,000, ANTALYA

15 October to 21 October 2018	Antalya, Turkey
ITF Women's Circuit	Surface: Hard
Main Draw	Entry: Direct Acceptance

Final	W	v Johana Marková (Czech Rep)	6–4, 6–2
Semi-final	W	v Alena Fomina-Klotz (Russia)	6–2, 6–3
Quarter-final	W	v Georgia Andreea Crăciun (Romania)	6–3, 6–2

2nd Round	W	v Polina Gubina (Ukraine)	6–3, 6–4
1st Round	W	v Arina Solomatina (Russia)	6–1, 6–3

ITF/TENNIS EUROPE $25,000, WIRRAL

29 October to 4 November 2018   Wirral, Great Britain
ITF Women's Circuit   Surface: Hard (indoor)
Main Draw   Entry: Wild Card

Semi-final	L	v Diāna Marcinkēviča (Latvia)	5–7, 1–6
Quarter-final	W	v Greet Minnen (Belgium)	7–6⁵, 6–2
2nd Round	W	v Barbara Haas (Austria)	3–6, 6–3, 6–2
1st Round	W	v Ayla Aksu (Turkey)	6–4, 6–1

2019

ITF/TENNIS EUROPE $25,000, GLASGOW

18 February to 24 February 2019   Glasgow, Great Britain
ITF World Tennis Tour   Surface: Hard (indoor)
Main Draw   Entry: Wild Card

2nd Round	L	v Valeria Savinykh (Russia)	6–1, 3–6, 4–6
1st Round	W	v Gabriela Lee (Romania)	6–3, 6–7⁵, 6–3

ITF $15,000, TEL AVIV

25 March to 31 March 2019   Tel Aviv, Israel
ITF World Tennis Tour   Surface: Hard
Main Draw   Entry: Direct Acceptance

Final	L	v Corinna Dentoni (Italy)	4–6, 3–6
Semi-final	W	v Vlada Ekshibarova (Israel)	7–6⁴, 5–7, 6–3
Quarter-final	W	v Marianna Zakarlyuk (Ukraine)	6–3, 5–7, 7–6³
2nd Round	W	v Sabrina Kalandarov (Israel)	6–1, 6–3
1st Round	W	v Maya Tahan (Israel)	2–6, 6–1, 6–3

ITF/TENNIS EUROPE $25,000, BOLTON

1 April to 7 April 2019		Bolton, Great Britain	
ITF World Tennis Tour		Surface: Hard (indoor)	
Main Draw		Entry: Special Exempt	
Semi-final	L	v Jodie Anna Burrage (GB)	6–2, 1–6, 4–6
Quarter-final	W	v Paula Badosa (Spain)	6–1, 6–2
2nd Round	W	v Robin Anderson (USA)	4–6, 6–3, 6–2
1st Round	W	v Laura-Ioana Paar (Romania)	6–4, 6–3

THE CHAMPIONSHIPS, WIMBLEDON

1 July to 14 July 2019		Wimbledon, Great Britain	
Grand Slam		Surface: Grass	
Qualifying Draw		Entry: Wild Card	
1st Round	L	v En Shuo Liang (Taipei)	6–7⁴, 2–6

ITF/TENNIS EUROPE $25,000, ROEHAMPTON (1)

16 September to 22 September 2019		Roehampton, Great Britain	
ITF World Tennis Tour		Surface: Hard	
Main Draw		Entry: Direct Acceptance	
Quarter-final	L	v Vivian Heisen (Germany)	5–7, 1–4 (retired)
2nd Round	W	v Leonie Kung (Switzerland)	6–2, 0–6, 6–2
1st Round	W	v Emily Arbuthnott (GB)	6–1, 6–3

ITF/TENNIS EUROPE $25,000, ROEHAMPTON (2)

23 September to 29 September 2019		Roehampton, Great Britain	
ITF World Tennis Tour		Surface: Hard	
Main Draw		Entry: Wild Card	
Semi-final	L	v Anna-Lena Friedsam (Germany)	4–6, 2–6
Quarter-final	W	v Susan Bandecchi (Switzerland)	7–5, 6–3
2nd Round	W	v Myrtille Georges (France)	7–5, 2–6, 7–5
1st Round	W	v Chanelle Van Nguyen (USA)	6–3, 6–2

ITF/TENNIS EUROPE $25,000, MINSK

11 November to 17 November 2019		Minsk, Belarus	
ITF World Tennis Tour		Surface: Hard (indoor)	
Main Draw		Entry: Qualifier	
Quarter-final	L	v Anastasia Zakharova (Russia)	5–7, 2–6
2nd Round	W	v Lara Salden (Belgium)	6–4, 7–5
1st Round	W	v Deborah Chiesa (Italy)	6–2, 6–0
Qualifying Draw		Entry: Direct Acceptance	
2nd Round	W	v Katyarina Paulenka (Belarus)	6–1, 6–4
1st Round	W	v Ekaterina Reyngold (Russia)	6–4, 6–2

ITF $25,000, SOLAPUR

2 December to 8 December 2019		Solapur, India	
ITF World Tennis Tour		Surface: Hard	
Main Draw		Entry: Direct Acceptance	
2nd Round	L	v Katie Boulter (GB)	2–6, 1–2 (retired)
1st Round	W	v Despina Papamichail (Greece)	6–2, 6–1

ITF $25,000, PUNE

9 December to 15 December 2019		Pune, India	
ITF World Tennis Tour		Surface: Hard	
Main Draw		Entry: Qualifier	
Final	W	v Naiktha Bains (GB)	3–6, 6–1, 6–4
Semi-final	W	v Olga Doroshina (Russia)	6–2, 4–6, 6–3
Quarter-final	W	v Shalimar Talbi (Belarus)	6–1, 5–7, 6–3
2nd Round	W	v Ulrikke Eikeri (Norway)	6–3, 6–0
1st Round	W	v Valeriya Strakhova (Ukraine)	6–0, 6–0
Qualifying Draw		Entry: Direct Acceptance	
2nd Round	W	v Jia-Qi Kang (China)	6–4, 6–1
1st Round	W	v Akanksha Dileep Nitture (India)	6–1, 6–0

2020

ITF/TENNIS EUROPE $25,000, GLASGOW

17 February to 23 February 2020		Glasgow, Great Britain
ITF World Tennis Tour		Surface: Hard (indoor)
Main Draw		Entry: Wild Card
1st Round	L v Marie Benoît (Belgium)	6–2, 2–2 (retired)

ITF/TENNIS EUROPE $25,000, SUNDERLAND

24 February to 1 March 2020		Sunderland, Great Britain
ITF World Tennis Tour		Surface: Hard (indoor)
Main Draw		Entry: Direct Acceptance
Final	L v Viktoriya Tomova (Bulgaria)	6–4, 4–6, 3–6
Semi-final	W v Clara Tauson (Denmark)	6–4, 6–2
Quarter-final	W v Richèl Hogenkamp (Netherlands)	6–3, 6–2
2nd Round	W v Amarni Banks (GB)	7–5, 6–3
1st Round	W v Elitsa Kostova (Bulgaria)	7–5, 6–1

2021

VIKING OPEN NOTTINGHAM

7 June to 13 June 2021		Nottingham, Great Britain
International		Surface: Grass
Main Draw		Entry: Wild Card
1st Round	L v Harriet Dart (GB)	3–6, 4–6

ITF/TENNIS EUROPE $100,000 + H, NOTTINGHAM

14 June to 20 June 2021		Nottingham, Great Britain
ITF World Tennis Tour		Surface: Grass
Main Draw		Entry: Wild Card
Quarter-final	L v Tsvetana Pironkova (Bulgaria)	5–7, 6–7^2
2nd Round	W v Tímea Babos (Hungary)	6–3, 6–3
1st Round	W v Storm Sanders (Australia)	7–6^3, 6–2

THE CHAMPIONSHIPS, WIMBLEDON

28 June to 11 July 2021		Wimbledon, Great Britain	
Grand Slam		Surface: Grass	
Main Draw		Entry: Wild Card	
4th Round	L	v Ajla Tomljanović (Australia)	4–6, 0–3 (retired)
3rd Round	W	v Sorana Cîrstea (Romania)	6–3, 7–5
2nd Round	W	v Markéta Vondroušová (Czech Rep)	6–2, 6–4
1st Round	W	v Vitalia Diatchenko (Russia)	7–6^4, 6–0

MUBADALA SILICON VALLEY CLASSIC, SAN JOSE

2 August to 8 August 2021		San Jose, USA	
Premier 700		Surface: Hard	
Main Draw		Entry: Wild Card	
1st Round	L	v Zhang Shuai (China)	3–6, 2–6

ITF W100, LANDISVILLE

9 August to 15 August 2021		Landisville, USA	
ITF World Tennis Tour		Surface: Hard	
Main Draw		Entry: Qualifier	
Quarter-final	L	v Nuria Párrizas Díaz (Spain)	3–4 (retired)
2nd Round	W	v Ekaterine Gorgodze (Georgia)	3–6, 6–0, 6–1
1st Round	W	v Ysaline Bonaventure (Belgium)	7–6^4, 6–2
Qualifying Draw		Entry: Direct Acceptance	
2nd Round	W	v Mona Barthel (Germany)	6–2, 6–3
1st Round	W	v Na-Lae Han (South Korea)	6–3, 6–0

WTA CHICAGO 125

16 August to 22 August 2021		Chicago, USA	
WTA $125,000 Series		Surface: Hard	
Main Draw		Entry: Wild Card	
Final	L	v Clara Tauson (Denmark)	1–6, 6–2, 4–6
Semi-final	W	v Claire Liu (USA)	7–6^3, 4–6, 6–1
Quarter-final	W	v Jule Niemeier (Germany)	7–6^4 (retired)

| 2nd Round | W | v Clara Burel (France) | 6–2, 7–5 |
| 1st Round | W | v Alison Van Uytvanck (Belgium) | 7–6⁷, 6–3 |

US OPEN

30 August to 12 September 2021			Flushing Meadows, NY, USA
Grand Slam			Surface: Hard
Main Draw			Entry: Qualifier
Final	W	v Leylah Fernandez (Canada)	6–4, 6–3
Semi-final	W	v Maria Sakkari (Greece)	6–1, 6–4
Quarter-final	W	v Belinda Bencic (Switzerland)	6–3, 6–4
4th Round	W	v Shelby Rogers (USA)	6–2, 6–1
3rd Round	W	v Sara Sorribes Tormo (Spain)	6–0, 6–1
2nd Round	W	v Zhang Shuai (China)	6–2, 6–4
1st Round	W	v Stefanie Voegele (Switzerland)	6–2, 6–3
Qualifying Draw			Entry: Direct Acceptance
3rd Round	W	v Mayar Sherif (Egypt)	6–1, 6–4
2nd Round	W	v Mariam Bolkvadze (Georgia)	6–3, 7–5
1st Round	W	v Bibiane Schoofs (Netherlands)	6–1, 6–2

BNP PARIBAS OPEN, INDIAN WELLS

4 October to 17 October 2021			Indian Wells, USA
Premier Mandatory			Surface: Hard
Main Draw			Entry: Wild Card
2nd Round	L	v Aliaksandra Sasnovich (Belarus)	2–6, 4–6
1st Round	Bye		

TRANSYLVANIA OPEN

25 October to 31 October 2021			Cluj Napoca, Romania
International			Surface: Hard (indoor)
Main Draw			Entry: Direct Acceptance
Quarter-final	L	v Marta Kostyuk (Ukraine)	2–6, 1–6
2nd Round	W	v Ana Bogdan (Romania)	6–3, 6–4
1st Round	W	v Polona Hercog (Slovenia)	4–6, 7–5, 6–1

UPPER AUSTRIA LADIES, LINZ

8 November to 14 November 2021		Linz, Austria
International		Surface: Hard (indoor)
Main Draw		Entry: Wild Card
2nd Round	L v Wang Xinyu (China)	1–6, 7–6^0, 5–7
1st Round	Bye	

2022

SYDNEY TENNIS CLASSIC

10 January to 16 January 2022		Sydney, Australia
Premier 700		Surface: Hard (indoor)
Main Draw		Entry: Direct Acceptance
1st Round	L v Elena Rybakina (Kazakhstan)	0–6, 1–6

AUSTRALIAN OPEN

17 January to 30 January 2022		Melbourne, Australia
Grand Slam		Surface: Hard
Main Draw		Entry: Direct Acceptance
2nd Round	L v Danka Kovinić (Montenegro)	4–6, 6–4, 3–6
1st Round	W v Sloane Stephens (USA)	6–0, 2–6, 6–1

ACKNOWLEDGEMENTS |

Any sportswriter will tell you that there are times when this job is a privilege. Being there to see Emma Raducanu win the US Open – one of the great sporting tales of our age – was certainly a case in point.

In being able to relate this story I am grateful to numerous people, notably those who gave their time to talk to me, both on and off the record. John Dolan of the Lawn Tennis Association was especially helpful in putting me in touch with some of those who agreed to speak. I am aware I have not spoken to everyone on the long list of people who have helped Emma along the way, but I hope it is a rounded cross section.

Special thanks to all those at Hodder & Stoughton involved in the making of this book. I am naturally indebted to Roddy Bloomfield, the wisest of sports publishers, who made it all possible and was an inspiring guide throughout the process. I particularly wish to thank the rest of Roddy's team at Hodder. They include the reassuring presence of editor Morgan Springett, picture researcher Lesley Hodgson and my excellent copy editor Tim Waller, whose contribution and patience have been invaluable.

I am also grateful to my colleagues, both inside the *Daily Mail* and those who travel on the road, for their good humour and professionalism. And to my family, for their constant support and understanding.

PICTURE ACKNOWLEDGEMENTS |

The author and publisher would like to thank the following for permission to reproduce photographs:

Section One: TPN/Getty Images; Avalon/TopFoto; PA Images/ Alamy Stock Photo; Javier Garcia/Shutterstock; Clive Brunskill/ Getty Images; Jack Thomas/Getty Images; Alex Davidson/Getty Images; Nathan Stirk/Getty Images; Adam Davy – Pool/Getty Images; Reuters/Alamy Stock Photo; Alberto Pezzali/AP/ Shutterstock; AELTC /Jonathan Nackstrand/Pool/EPA-EFE/ Shutterstock; Javier Garcia/Shutterstock; Kirsty Wigglesworth/ AP/Shutterstock; Mal Taam/CSM/Shutterstock; Shutterstock.

Section Two: Matthew Stockman/Getty Images; Matthew Stockman/Getty Images; Justin Lane/EPA-EFE/Shutterstock; John G Mabanglo/EPA-EFE/Shutterstock; John G Mabanglo/ EPA-EFE/Shutterstock; Justin Lane/EPA-EFE/Shutterstock; Chine Nouvelle/SIPA/Shutterstock; Sarah Stier/Getty Images; Jason Szenes/EPA-EFE/Shutterstock; Sarah Stier/Getty Images; Elsa/Getty Images; Elsa/Getty Images; John G Mabanglo/ EPA-EFE/Shutterstock; Susan Mullane/Alamy Stock Photo;

Frank Franklin II/AP/Shutterstock; Matthew Stockman/Getty Images; Evan Agostini/Invision/AP/Shutterstock; PA Images/ Alamy Stock Photo; Chris Jackson/Getty Images; Clive Brunskill/Getty Images; Flaviu Buboi/NurPhoto via Getty Images; James Ross/EPA-EFE/Shutterstock.

Chapter Openers: Alex Davidson/Getty Images; Avalon/TopFoto; Julian Finney/Getty Images; Julian Finney/Getty Images; AELTC/ David Gray/Pool/AFP via Getty Images; Mal Taam/CSM/ Shutterstock; John G Mabanglo/EPA-EFE/Shutterstock; J. Conrad Williams. Jr./Newsday RM via Getty Images; David Rose/ Shutterstock; James D. Morgan/Getty Images.

INDEX